WHO AM I & WHY AM I HERE?

—8 REASONS GOD CREATED THE HUMAN RACE—

DR. BILL HAMON

Destiny Image® Publishers, Inc.
P.O. Box 310
Shippensburg, PA 17257-0310

"We Publish the Prophets"

ISBN 0-7684-2255-8

For Worldwide Distribution
Printed in the U.S.A.

This book and all other Destiny Image, Revival Press, MercyPlace,
Fresh Bread, Destiny Image Fiction, and Treasure House books are available
at Christian bookstores and distributors worldwide.

1 2 3 4 5 6 7 8 9 10 / 09 08 07 06 05

For a U.S. bookstore nearest you, call
1-800-722-6774.

For more information on foreign distributors, call
717-532-3040.

Or reach us on the Internet:
www.destinyimage.com

TABLE OF CONTENTS

INTRODUCTION

As you read this book you will discover truths about the purpose for mankind's existence on earth. Many of the things revealed have never been printed before but they are all based on biblical realities. Around 200 Scripture references are used to help the reader prove to himself that the ideas presented are according to the Bible. Hundreds more could have been given to prove their validity but this is not written to be a theological book. It is written in the form of a novel to make for more exciting and interesting reading.

Jesus Christ did most of His teaching with parables. A parable is a true-to-life story used to reveal a particular reality or truth. It is not mythology or fiction based on nonexistent things. A true parable may use proper names but not be speaking of a particular person or incident, but that type of person does exist and such incidents do take place. Who Am I and Why Am I Here could be called a hypothetical illustration based on true realities of God, angels, earth, Heaven, spirit beings, and mortal mankind.

The main characters' names were chosen for their practicality, not for their significance. There is a priestly prophet in the Bible named Eli. The first three letters of the names of two of the greatest prophets in the Bible are Eli—Elijah and Elisha. Randy is taken to see the prophet because God has enabled His prophets to know the secrets of God. Amos 3:7 declares, "Surely the Lord God does nothing, unless He reveals His secrets to His servants the prophets." What God plans to do on earth is revealed to and through those whom

God has gifted with His prophet anointing. More than 90 percent of the books of the Old Testament were written by Prophets.

Prophet Moses wrote the first five books of the Bible. They were written 2,500 years after Adam and Eve left the garden of Eden. How did Moses know the accurate details of the creation of Heaven and earth and mankind? In modern terminology we would probably say that God showed Moses a video playback of the whole thing while he was on Mount Sinai with God for 40 days and nights. However, I think the way it happened is similar to the way our main character in this book was taken back through time and space to a place before time began. He was privileged to see the unfolding history of earth and mankind. He saw the past just as in the New Testament Apostle John was taken into the timeless dimension of Heaven and shown the future of mankind until the end of mortal man and the end of the world as we know it today.

Apostle Paul in the New Testament states that the mysteries of God were made known by divine revelation and the understanding of these mysteries "which in other ages was not made known to the sons of men, as it has now been revealed by the Spirit to His holy apostles and prophets" (Eph. 3:5). Over half of the books of the New Testament were written by Apostle Paul. His teachings were so new and revolutionary to the religions of his day that he had to receive most of it by revelation and by being taken to that timeless dimension called paradise (see 2 Cor. 12:1-4). He was given understanding of the things he wrote in his epistles and even shown things that he was not allowed to write for man to read. I am explaining these truths so that the reader will see that there is biblical justification for presenting truth in the form used in this book.

In the 1960s I taught at a Christian College for five years. More than 500 students filled out a survey with one of the questions being, "Why did God create the human race?" Interestingly enough, 98 percent of all students gave the same answer—for fellowship or for worship or both. You can ask any Christian why God created mankind and most of them will give that same answer. Those are two reasons why God created mankind, but you will discover in reading this book that there are other reasons that are more major and meaningful to God. For example, you will understand why God planned the crucifixion of Jesus Christ and when He planned to create mankind. Most people understand what mankind received from Christ Jesus' death on the Cross—a way for sinful mankind to be forgiven and reconciled to God. But what did it do for God? What personal desire and purpose did it fulfill for God? When you grasp that reason it should make you understand and greatly appreciate Almighty God for being the God that He is. Some of the other reasons will make God more personal and real. I taught the students in our Ministry Training College these eight reasons God created the human race. I had them choose the one that was the most exciting and relevant to them. It was very interesting to see which one they chose and why it was more exciting and meaningful to them. I would love to know which reason will be the most enlightening, relevant, and exciting to you.

You should be convinced by the time you have discovered and understand all eight purposes that God had a reason for everything He created. He had a reason for making man's body from the dust of the earth; for making mankind male and female with the power of procreation; for placing man on planet earth, which was satan's and his fallen angels' place of imprisonment; for putting the forbidden tree of the knowledge of good and evil in the garden of Eden, which was man's paradise home; for sending the great flood; for waiting 4,000 years before coming to earth; and a reason why Jesus Christ has not returned to earth yet.

I pray for you the prayer that Apostle Paul prayed for the Ephesians Christians:

That the God of our Lord Jesus Christ, the Father of glory, may give to you the spirit of wisdom and revelation in the knowledge of Him, the eyes of your understanding being enlightened; that you may know what is the hope of His calling, what are the riches of the glory of His inheritance in the saints, and what is the exceeding greatness of His power toward us who believe, according to the working of His mighty power (Ephesians 1:17-19).

Enter now with our main character Randy into the land of revelation and wisdom so that at the end of the journey you can say with greater conviction and knowledge: Now I know more than ever before who I am and why I am here. *Now my life has more "reason and rhyme" and I understand why the world is the way it is. I will now live my life with greater meaning for now I know my purpose and destiny and what I must do and be for it to be fulfilled.*

You will never be the same after understanding eight of the major reasons for which you were created. You have purpose in your being and a wonderful destiny to fulfill.

1

A Brief History of Man

Thunder rattled the windows as Randy closed the door to his dorm room. Dropping his books on his desk he took off his jacket, shook the water off of it, hung it on the edge of his bed, and then plopped down heavily into his chair. For a few moments he gazed silently out the window. Gusts of strong wind spat rain against the glass in pelting sheets. Sharp barbs of lightning tore the gray, sunless, late afternoon sky, casting an eerie luminosity to the campus below. It was quite a thunderstorm. The late afternoon cloudburst had hit just as classes were ending for the afternoon, catching everyone by surprise and sending them scurrying in every direction to escape the sudden downpour. Watching the rain and the lightning and listening to the thunder reminded Randy once again of the awesome might and majesty of a God who could create a natural world capable of such a forceful display of raw power.

That thought brought Randy's attention back to his current dilemma. He turned and stared glumly for a few moments at his philosophy textbook lying on top of the stack on his desk. Another frustrating hour in Philosophy 101. As the only Christian in a room full of confirmed religious skeptics, Randy always found his philosophy class a challenge. And it was not only his philosophy class. Every day it seemed as though something he believed came under attack. Astronomy, biology, psychology; in every class his professors—and most of his classmates—simply assumed a naturalistic explanation for the origins of the universe, life, and of man himself. Even in his English class there were discussions that made it clear that any notions of a personal God who controlled the universe were considered archaic and naïve.

Randy had quickly discovered upon coming to college that it was one thing to *be* a Christian on campus but quite another to *defend* his beliefs against those who disagreed and were not bashful about saying so! He even suspected that some of his classmates had made a game of baiting him, deliberately making provocative statements to see if they could trip up the "religious nut" in their class.

How could he even begin to engage his fellow students on an equal footing when they seemed so confident, so self-assured, so…arrogant? Randy knew what he believed but the thought of trying to explain his beliefs in open debate scared him. What could he say? What proofs could he offer? He didn't have a clue.

With a heavy sigh, Randy pulled out his class notes. After today it was even worse. His philosophy professor had given the class an assignment to write a theme paper answering the question, "What is the purpose of man?" Randy wanted to write his paper from the perspective of his Christian faith even though he knew it would probably bring more ridicule raining down on his head. His problem was that he didn't know where to begin.

"What *is* the purpose of man?" Randy asked out loud. "Why on earth *are* we here?" He thought back, trying to remember sermons or Bible teachings he had heard on the subject at his church back home. One pastor, he recalled, had said that man was created to worship God and to have fellowship with Him. Randy quickly jotted that thought down in his notebook.

"That's all fine and good," Randy thought, "but that's hardly enough to write a whole theme paper on. Isn't there something more? Were we placed on this earth only to worship and have fellowship with God, or did He have a greater purpose in mind?"

The more Randy thought about man's purpose on earth, the more the subject intrigued him, and the more he wanted to come up with an answer from the Bible and the Christian perspective that would stand up under the examination of even the most critical skeptics in his class. Clearing off his desk, Randy pulled out his Bible and opened it to the

Book of Genesis. Beginning at the beginning, he slowly read through the first three chapters, writing down notes and observations as he went along. Then, using his concordance and his Bible's cross-referencing system, he read every verse he could find that referred to mankind or to God's purpose for creating the human race.

Minutes stretched into hours as Randy lost himself in the study, reading and comparing verses, and writing notes furiously. Finally, when the words in front of him started to blur, Randy dropped his pen on his notebook, sat back and rubbed his bleary eyes. After his eyes cleared, he picked up his notebook and skimmed through the ten pages of notes he had written. There were many Scripture references and plenty of personal observations and questions, but they still had not come together in any logical or sensible way in his mind. He still could not quite see the connection. In some ways, Randy felt that he didn't understand any more now about God's purpose for man than when he had started.

Randy glanced at the clock on the corner of his desk. 2:30 A.M. He had worked straight through dinner and hours beyond. Surrendering to fatigue and frustration, Randy leaned forward and lowered his head to rest on his crossed arms on the desk. "What does it all mean, Lord?" he prayed. "I don't understand! Why did You create us? What are we here for? Help me!" No sooner had the words of Randy's prayer left his lips than he was asleep.

Suddenly, Randy was surrounded by a brilliant light, a light so bright that he could see it even through his closed eyelids. Then he heard a voice call out to him. "Randy."

Opening his eyes and sitting up, Randy was surprised that the light, as brilliant as it was, did not hurt his eyes. Brightness was everywhere, washing out everything around him. He could feel the chair under him and the desk under his arms, but he could not see them. At first he could see nothing at all. Then, out of the midst of the light, the voice came again. "Randy."

"Who are you?" Randy asked, a slight tremor in his voice.

The brilliance of the light subsided somewhat and Randy saw before him a tall figure in a flowing garment that stretched from its neck to its feet, a garment of shimmering colors that swirled and changed as the being walked toward him. In its shining face the figure appeared human and yet not quite human, neither young nor old, but essentially ageless. Its piercing eyes held Randy in a gaze that made him feel that he was looking into the threshold of eternity.

As the being stood silently before him with its radiant and penetrating countenance focused on him, Randy managed to ask a second time, "Who are you?"

In a voice with the richness of thundering waterfalls, the being answered, "I am Raphael."[1]

"R-R-Raphael," Randy stammered. His heart hammered from fear. He had a sudden urge to flee but all strength had left him and he felt like he could not even stand up, much less run. Barely able to speak, his next question came out as little more than a squeak. "So, you're an angel, then?"

Raphael's visage was unchanged as he answered. "A messenger of the Most High God, yes."

"What do you want?" Randy asked in a whisper.

"Don't be afraid, Randy," the archangel replied. "God has heard your prayer and has sent me for you."

Randy swallowed a couple of times. He was starting to get his voice back. "He sent you for me? What does that mean? I don't understand."

"The King of Heaven has afforded you a rare and unique privilege—an eyewitness view of the beginning."

"The beginning? Of what?"

"The beginning of all things."

"I'm sorry," Randy said, shaking his head, "but I'm still confused."

"You wish to understand God's purpose for mankind. God heard your prayer and is pleased with your desire. He wants you to understand and has decided to show you. The best way to do that is to start at the beginning."

Randy's fear was gone now, but a sense of amazement had taken its place. "You mean we're going to go there? How is that possible? It happened so long ago!"

"Is anything impossible for God?" Raphael asked.

Overwhelmed with astonishment, Randy did not respond. Raphael reached toward him. "Here, Randy. Take my hand. Don't be afraid. Come with me and you will learn everything you need to know."

Almost as if in a trance, Randy slowly held out his hand, never taking his eyes off of Raphael's face. The tall, shining archangel took Randy's hand into his own. Immediately, Randy felt himself rising from his chair. They continued to rise, through the ceiling, through the roof of the dormitory and into the night sky. In a daze, Randy watched the ground drop away below him. Faster and faster through the air they ascended, yet there was no wind, and no sense of gravity. They were soaring free with nothing at all to resist their flight.

In a matter of moments they were high enough for Randy to make out the curvature of the earth. The sky steadily darkened as they approached the lower edge of space. As the atmosphere thinned, the stars in the heavens became clearer and sharper than he had ever seen from earth. Pictures he had seen of the earth taken from space could not compare to the stunning beauty of the bluish-green land and seascape stretched out below him.

Caught up in the wonderment of what he was seeing, Randy was only vaguely aware of the fact that although apparently surrounded by the vacuum of space, he was still able to breathe. Somehow, he reasoned, as soon as he had taken hold of Raphael's hand, he had been translated into another dimension, another reality, another realm that was not bound by the laws of time and space.

As Randy and Raphael continued to fly outward, the earth beneath them diminished in relative size until it occupied only about one-fourth of the sky. Then they stopped moving and Randy saw that they were now hovering motionless relative to the planet and thousands of miles above its surface. Raphael remained silent and still, as if he was waiting for something. After a few moments, Randy looked at the archangel and asked, "What now?"

"Watch."

As Randy continued to observe the bluish-green world below him, his eyes detected some details he hadn't noticed before. He saw the terminator, the line delineating night and day, and the sea and land mass of the earth moving under it from the planet's rotation. Something about it didn't look quite right, however. As he watched, the west coast of North America emerged from under the darkness and moved westward away from the terminator. It seemed to Randy that the motion was too easy to see—too fast—as if he was watching a video at high speed. There was something else though…suddenly he had it! North America was retreating to the west. That meant that the terminator was moving *west to east*!

"Raphael," Randy asked, "what's happening?"

"What do your senses tell you, Randy?"

"The rotation is all wrong! It's going in the wrong direction! The earth is moving *backward*!"

"A very astute observation," Raphael replied. "However, in this case your senses have deceived you. The earth is not moving backward—*we* are."

"*We're* moving backward?"

"In time."

The speed of the earth's "reverse" spin began to increase, faster and faster until the surface was nothing but a blur. With clockwork precision, the moon circled the earth with ever increasing speed, its phases changing rapidly as it kept one side facing the earth. Randy and Raphael continued to "move" back in time, faster and faster. Now Randy could see the earth's characteristic "wobble" as the angle of its axis toward the sun changed with the changing of the seasons. To Randy's mind it resembled a child's toy top nearing the end of its spin, as it wobbles just before falling over. Centuries flew by in a moment's time, ticking off like the seconds on a clock. Finally, after what seemed like hours, although Randy knew intuitively that only a few minutes had passed, the speed of motion began to decrease. Slower and slower the earth's rotation became until it seemed to stop entirely.

Randy gasped in amazement. The surface of the earth looked completely different. Gone were the familiar outlines of Europe, Asia, and the Americas that he knew from maps and geography textbooks. All the land mass of the planet was gathered together in one place, forming a single, giant "super continent." There were no signs anywhere of clouds of any kind. Randy also noticed that no ice was visible anywhere on the surface. Even the north and south poles were ice-free. Something was strange too about the region of space right around the earth. It seemed different; empty somehow. Suddenly he realized why: the moon was nowhere to be seen.

"Raphael, how far back have we come?"

"Far enough for you to get the answers you seek."

"But what happened to the earth? It looks so different."

"You are seeing the earth as it was long before mankind first inhabited it, a time so remote that it is all but beyond human imagination. The earth appears different to you because it is different. It is not the same world you live in. This world had to be recreated to become the world you know."

"Why?" Randy asked. "What happened?"

"Keep watching," the tall archangel replied. "You'll find out."

Suddenly Randy noticed that they were moving again. This time it really was them moving. The strange-looking "earth" before him remained as it was, but Randy and the angel were now descending toward a brightly lit area directly below them that seemed to be suspended in space. The light was brilliant and radiant in quality, definitely other-worldly to Randy's eyes, and it seemed to pulsate with a richness that Randy could describe only as the glory of God. Somehow, he knew intuitively that they were approaching Heaven.

Drawing closer, Randy perceived through the bright light objects that resembled towers and battlements, reminding him of pictures of medieval castles he had seen in his history books. Their descent was taking them toward a large, open courtyard-like area that had what appeared to be a richly carved stone balustrade at the outer edge. Overall, the place looked like an enormous balcony.

Slowly they descended until their feet touched lightly down on the stone-like surface of the courtyard. Randy looked up at the tall archangel. "Raphael," he began, "is this…"

"Yes, Randy. This is the palace of our Master, the King and Lord of the universe."

"Does it *really* look like this?" Everything around him glowed with that pulsating, radiant light. Behind him, the walls of the palace stretched up and up until they were lost in the brilliance of the illumination. He could not even see the top.

"That is an interesting question," the archangel replied. "You see what your senses are prepared to see—all that your finite human mind is capable of comprehending. What you need to understand, Randy, is that everything in this realm is bigger, richer, and fuller in every dimension than you can perceive with your limited earthly senses. Someday, when you leave your earthly existence to live eternally in this realm, you will see fully and clearly. Until then, you will have to accept what your senses tell you."

They walked to the edge of the courtyard and Randy looked out over the balustrade at the strange blue planet swimming below. "Is there anything down there?" he asked. "I mean, any life?"

In answer, with a suddenness that took Randy's breath away, the planet's surface leaped toward him as if he were viewing it through the zoom lens of a camera. Details became sharper and clearer. He saw plants and trees of odd design that looked totally alien to him. Among them moved a myriad of creatures, some small and scampering, others large and lumbering. It took him a few moments to recognize them.

"Dinosaurs!" Randy said in astonishment.

"Yes," Raphael confirmed, "but that's not all. Listen."

At first, Randy heard nothing. After a few moments, as he continued to listen, his ears caught the first faint strains of music rising from the earth's surface. The longer he listened, the clearer and louder the music became until it was like a symphony in his ears. It was like no music Randy had ever heard before. It reminded him of organ music, but different; like a full orchestra of wind instruments, yet beyond anything he had ever heard on earth. Melody and harmony seemed to wrap themselves around him, lifting his spirit to a sudden explosion of joy. The music penetrated to the very core of his being, stunningly and seductively beautiful and, to Randy's mind, utterly unearthly.

Stunned almost beyond words, Randy managed to whisper, "I hear music! Where is it coming from?" As soon as he said this, the view of the earth receded to its original proportions.

"From the earth," Raphael answered. "You are looking at the jurisdictional regency of lucifer, the highest of God's anointed cherubim, master of all pipes and music, and leader in heaven of the worship of the Most High God. Lucifer, along with his host of angelic aides, oversees this galaxy—the one you call the Milky Way. Earth is his headquarters."

"Lucifer! You mean satan—the devil?"

Raphael was silent for a few moments as if pondering his reply. His face was inscrutable, his eyes distant as if he was remembering something significant from long ago. Finally, he said simply, "The devil? No, not yet. Soon. Come with me, Randy. There is something else you must see."

Turning away from the railing, Raphael began making his way across the courtyard with Randy following. They were approaching the entrance to a large room from which, as they drew nearer, Randy could hear voices. Upon entering the great room, Randy's eyes were immediately drawn to an enormous dais in the center, which rose hundreds of feet above the floor. Its crest was awash in the same radiant light that illuminated everything else, but here it was strongest of all, pulsating with power, majesty, and indescribable beauty. It was obvious to Randy that here was the source for the light of Heaven. A rainbow, completely circular and the color of emerald surrounded the top of the dais. Through the pulsating brilliance of the light, Randy caught glimpses of what appeared to be a throne and the form of Someone seated on it. Because of the brightness of the light, he could not make out any features. Around the throne, countless seraphim cried out,

"Holy, holy, holy, is the Lord God Almighty." A myriad of other angels was flying to and fro carrying out the will of their King.

Suddenly, an overwhelming sense of awe swept over Randy. He became intensely aware of the holiness of this place and of the One who sat on the throne—and of his own littleness. He felt dirty and out of place, unfit to be where he was. Struck speechless, and almost unaware of himself, Randy fell to his knees and bowed his face to the floor in abject humility and reverent worship.

As Randy lay prostrate before the King, the sense of awe and reverent fear that had overwhelmed him so quickly was itself suddenly supplanted by a wave of warm benevolence that seemed to fill every cell of his body. His spirit leaped inside him as the deepest, richest, purest, and fullest sense of absolute love that he had ever known covered him like a blanket.

Caught up as he was in the fullness of the glory and love of God, Randy lost track of how long he lay there before the throne. After a while, however, he sensed a change in the environment. The myriad voices of the seraphim ceased, and as Randy raised his head, it seemed as though the entire heavenly court had grown silent, listening and waiting.

A thunderous voice spoke from the throne, a voice that vibrated with life, power, authority, and infinite goodness.

"It has begun," the voice boomed. "Lucifer has made his move. I anticipated this. Michael."

At the summons, an archangel separated himself from the host in service around the throne, flew down to the foot of the throne and knelt there. Michael was similar in appearance to Raphael except that he had a long sword at his side.

When Michael was kneeling before Him, the King said, "Michael, you know what to do."

"Yes, my Lord," Michael replied. Immediately, he arose and flew off through the entrance to the throne room.

"Michael?" Randy asked, looking up at Raphael.

"Yes," the angel answered, "the captain of the angelic army of Heaven."

"What's going to happen now?"

"Come with me and you will see. You must not miss this."

Randy followed Raphael back out into the courtyard and over to the balustrade that overlooked the earth. At first, Randy saw and heard nothing. As he continued to watch the slowly turning planet beneath him, a sudden loud scream made him jump. The scream seemed to be filled with rage and utter anguish. After rising to a high pitch it began to trail off. Just then Randy saw a fiery red light vault over the edge of Heaven and streak toward the earth like a meteor. Immediately, countless other voices rose up in wails of helpless despair, and numberless thousands of lesser red streaks hurtled downward after the first on a collision course with the planet below.

The earth lit up from the effect of multiplied thousands of silent impacts. Then, even as Randy watched, the terminator shadow swept across from east to west with incredible speed until a thick darkness engulfed the entire planet. The darkness was so deep and moved so quickly that the earth appeared to simply wink out of existence from the night sky. After a few moments, however, Randy caught glimpses here and there of light reflecting dimly from the surface, enough for him to see that the planet was now encased in solid ice.

Randy was shocked beyond comprehension. In unbelief he turned to the tall archangel by his side, "Raphael, what...what happened? What does this mean?"

"Isn't it clear to you, Randy?" Raphael answered. "Lucifer led a revolt against God. He and the angels who followed him—one-third of our total company—stormed the gates of Heaven in an effort to dethrone the Most High God. It was lucifer's aim to set himself equal to God and to rule in His place. His pride blinded him to the utter futility of such a plan. He failed, of course."

"Then those bright red streaks like meteors were lucifer and his followers falling to earth, just as I have read in my Bible?"

"Yes. Michael and the angelic host met them at the gates, turned them back in total defeat, and cast them out of Heaven."

"What happened to them?"

"They are bound in an abyss prepared especially for them. In the very place where they conspired against God, they are bound just as securely as the planet itself is bound in ice. There they shall remain for a long time."

"How long?"

"Millions of your years. Until the fullness of time has come in the Almighty's plan. Then they will be released. Even in rebellion, lucifer has a role yet to play in the King's design. *Now* you are correct, Randy. *Now* lucifer has become satan—the devil. From now on he will be the sworn adversary of the Almighty and all who believe in Him; the accuser of all who look to God as their Father."

"I'm puzzled, Raphael," Randy said. "Everything I've seen up to now predates the appearance of man on the earth?"

"Yes. What you have seen so far occurred long before the world you know was fashioned and formed. The cataclysmic disaster of lucifer's rebellion and fall so distorted and altered the earth that it must be unmade and recreated before it will be ready for humankind."

"That's what I don't understand. I can't fit any of this that I have just seen into my understanding of creation."

"Go back to your Bible, Randy," Raphael said. "What does it say about creation?"

"It says, 'In the beginning God created the heavens and the earth.'"[2]

"And the next part?"

Randy thought for a moment. "'Now the earth was (or became) formless and empty, darkness was over the surface of the deep, and the Spirit of God was hovering over the waters.'"[3]

"Correct. Now, the first part has to do with the original creation. What does the second part deal with?"

The light of understanding was beginning to dawn in Randy's brain. "The *re*-creation of the earth in preparation for the creation of man?"

"Correct again," Raphael said. "So in which part do you fit what you have just seen?"

"I don't know; I guess it really fits in the middle."

"Exactly. What you saw just now occurred in the time *between* the first and second parts."

"But Raphael," Randy said, "you told me the earth would be in this state for millions of years. That's a long time."

"In your world, yes," the archangel replied. "Remember that you must look at this from the viewpoint of the heavenly realm where time as you understand it has no meaning. Such a large interval of time is nothing compared to eternity."

Randy nodded with understanding. "Does that mean the next step is the remaking of the earth?"

"Indeed it does."

"Will I get to see it?" Randy asked excitedly.

"That's why you are here, Randy."

"How long will I have to wait?"

"Patience, Randy. Actually, it is just about time right now."

"But how...?" Randy began. "What about all those millions of years?"

"They have been passing as we speak. Don't forget that time means nothing here."

At that moment the sound of praise and music from the throne room got louder. Randy and the archangel turned to see a procession of cherubim, seraphim, and lesser angels walking through the enormous entryway into the courtyard. There were thousands of them, singing and praising God as they came. To Randy's ears, the music sounded even more beautiful and glorious than lucifer's music he had heard earlier. At the very center of the processional walked the King of kings Himself, His features still hidden from Randy's view by the brilliant, holy light that emanated from Him. Again Randy felt the irresistible urge to drop to his knees in worship.

As soon as he did so, the same wave of warm and intense love he had felt earlier in the throne room swept over him once again. This time, he heard a voice speaking into his spirit. "Arise, Randy. Come and see what I am about to do, for that is why you were brought here."

Slowly, Randy rose to his feet and walked to the balustrade and stood at the outer edge of the angelic audience. The voice spoke to him again. "Come closer, Randy." Encouraged by Raphael at his side, Randy slowly made his way forward. None of the other angels in the heavenly host acknowledged his presence in any way.

"Do they see me?" Randy asked Raphael. "Do they even know I am here?"

"No, they do not," the archangel answered. "That is by the King's desire. He has allowed you a look into your remote past to see things as they were—as they are *now* from the heavenly perspective."

"All this happened in the past, but is also happening *now*? I don't understand."

"Your earthly existence is bound by the constraints of time— past, present, and future. It is different in Heaven. In this eternal realm there is no past, present, or future; there is only *now*."

"*You* see me."

"Of course. I was sent to bring you here and to be your guide."

"And the King knows I'm here."

"Certainly. The King knows all things, and He is the One who sent me to you."

Randy wanted to ask more questions, but by now he and Raphael had reached the inner edge of the circle surrounding the King, a circle that maintained a respectful and reverential distance from Him. The entire company of angels grew silent in anticipation of what was to come. Everyone, including Randy, had their eyes fixed on the dark, frozen planet barely visible below them.

The King spoke in a voice like thunder. "I am going to make a new creature; a creature that will be unique—completely different from any other creature I have made." Long moments of silence followed as the King stood motionless. It seemed to Randy as though He was brooding over what He was about to do.

Then, addressing the cosmos before Him, the King spoke again. "Let there be light!"[4] Instantly, light sprang forth and illuminated the barren, frozen earth below them as if a great lamp had been switched on. Darkness fled all around. The light seemed to emanate from everywhere, unfocused, with no visible coherent source. Randy was awestruck by what he was seeing. The King of creation considered the light for a moment then said, "That's good!"[5] He then differentiated between the darkness and the light. "Whenever the darkness prevails it shall be called 'Night'; whenever the light prevails it shall be called 'Day.'"[6]

Again the King spoke. "Let there be an expanse between the waters to separate water from water."[7] Immediately the thick ice encasing the earth began to thaw and to boil away, evaporating until much of it was in the atmosphere and formed a thick mist or cloud cover that completely obscured the surface.

As earlier, the earth suddenly expanded in size as though they were drawing closer and descending through the mist. Very soon the mist cleared and Randy could see that what water remained from the thawing now covered the surface of the earth. The surface was only dimly lit, evidently due to the mist blocking the light from penetrating. From this vantage point, it appeared that they were suspended in the expanse between the cloud cover and the water. With a wave of His hand the King said, "This expanse that separates water from water shall be called 'Sky.'"[8]

The King stretched forth His hand once again, this time to the earth itself and said, "The earth must no longer be completely covered by water. Dry land, Arise! Water, form into oceans, seas and rivers."[9] Even as Randy watched, the waters on the surface of the earth separated from one another and a great land mass arose from the depths—the same "super continent" Randy had seen earlier. Then, as Randy gasped in amazement, the land mass seemed to break apart and the pieces moved away from each other across the water, finally settling into the familiar shapes he knew from geography: North and South America, joined in the middle by Mexico and the tiny isthmus of Panama. They did not look quite the same, however. Although Randy could see lakes and rivers and snow-capped mountains, all the land was dull and brown. There was no vegetation anywhere.

Once again the voice of the King boomed out. "The dry land shall be called 'Earth' and the gathering of the waters, 'Seas.'" Pausing for a moment, the King surveyed His handiwork, and then pronounced, "That's good!"[10] All the heavenly host gathered there responded in a great chorus, "Amen, O Lord, You do all things well!"

The King spoke again and said, "Let the earth bring forth vegetation: seed-bearing plants and fruit-bearing trees, each plant after its own kind and each with its own seed."[11] Entranced, Randy watched as green vegetation appeared at the edges of the lakes and along the banks of the rivers, then spread out rapidly over the land. In a matter of moments the barren brown earth was completely blanketed with lush plant life.

Randy thought he caught a whiff of the sweet smell of flowers. "Is it possible?" he asked himself. He looked up at Raphael. "Do I smell the plant life of earth—from *here*?" he whispered. Raphael said nothing but simply nodded his head.

It must have been true, because the King paused for a few moments, as if savoring the aroma Himself, then proclaimed with satisfaction, "A-a-h-h-h-h! That's good!"[12]

The King's next move was to consolidate the unfocused light that bathed the earth. "Let there be lights in the expanse of the sky to separate the day from the night, to mark seasons and years, and to give light upon the earth.[13] Mist, roll back and allow the sun's rays to break through as well as the light from the billions upon billions of stars in My vast universe." Immediately, the earth's surface began to brighten as the mist dissolved. For the first time since his arrival, Randy saw the sun as a coherent object in the sky.

With another wave of His hand, the King set the earth to spinning on its axis. The land masses, stationary before, now began moving as the planet attained rotational speed. Although he could only barely detect the movement from this distance, Randy knew from his science studies that the earth was rotating at the speed of 1,040 miles per hour. The moon reappeared also as the Lord of Creation set it within its correct orbital relationship to its mother planet. Then the Lord said, "The greater light—the sun—will govern the day while the lesser light—the moon—will govern the night."[14] After watching the orderly exchange of night and day and the heavenly bodies in their courses, He said, "That's good!"[15]

After this, God stretched His hands out over the sky and over the seas and the rivers and the lakes and commanded, "Let the water teem with living creatures, and let birds fly above the earth across the expanse of the sky."[16] Instantly, billions of creatures filled the waters, from the tiniest algae to the mammoth whales. Birds of every description gathered in flocks so dense that they darkened the skies. Randy had seen migratory birds in formation before, but never anything like this. The sheer numbers staggered his imagination. Once again, God said, "That's good!"[17]

Michael, who had joined the throng after returning from his engagement with lucifer and his forces, inquired of God, "Master, which of these is the new creature you said you would make?"

"None of them," the King answered. "All of these creatures will be for the use and pleasure of my new, special creation. My new creature will live on the land and breathe the air."

Speaking to the earth once more, the King commanded, "Let the land produce living creatures according to their kinds: livestock, creatures that move along the ground, and wild animals, each according to its kind."[18] As with the seas and the sky, the land instantly swarmed with all sorts of living creatures: lizards and lions and leopards, sheep and cattle and horses, dogs and cats, foxes and rats, apes and elephants—millions of species. The sheer breadth and depth of God's creativity left Randy in awe. Of the animals and this phase of His creative plan, God said, "That's good!"

"Lord," another angel asked, "is one of these your special creation?"

Again God answered, "No. These too will be for the benefit and pleasure of My new special creature. All of the creatures you see here were spoken into existence. I have a different process in mind for My special creature."

Michael spoke up again. "Master, what is Your purpose in creating this new creature?" Randy's ears perked up upon hearing Michael's question.

The King replied, "Through this new race of beings I will bring forth new revelations and understanding of My nature and character. I will also do a thing in their midst that has never been done before. The feat that I will perform will leave an everlasting memorial for all generations that I am a God of love. I will start by placing My new creature here on the earth, where lucifer began his revolt against Me."

"But Lord," Michael said, "would it not be best if we removed lucifer and his host to another part of the universe and forbid them ever to contact this sphere?"

"No!" the King answered emphatically. "Lucifer will remain here. My new, special creature will be created in My own image and likeness and will be endowed with the power of choice. I want neither blind obedience nor mechanical worship and service. I want this new creature to do My will freely out of personal desire."

All of Heaven grew completely quiet again in anticipation of what would happen next. Randy was concentrating so intensely on the scene that he was not even aware that he was scarcely breathing.

"Watch," the King of Heaven declared, "and see what I will do! I shall now bring forth My Masterpiece. I will make 'Man' in My own image and likeness and he will rule over the fish of the sea, the birds of the air, and all the creatures that move on the ground.[19] I will not speak him into existence as I did with the other creatures, but will fashion him with My own hands."

Speaking then to the earth, God said, "You shall be the mother of the first man, for from you shall come the substance from which his body shall be made."

God then reached down, scooped up a big heap of red clay-like dirt from the earth, and began sculpting it in His hands. Randy, Raphael, and the entire heavenly host watched in rapt silence as the very image of the King took shape in the clay.[20] He pressed it and stretched it and molded it until it took the form of a body that generally resembled Randy's, complete in every way from the microscopic molecules to the mighty muscles, from the mysterious brain to the masterful bone structure, from the intricate nervous system to the circulatory system with its heart and miles of blood vessels, to the respiratory system with its powerful lungs; as many as 75 trillion cells in all.

When the King had finished His sculpting work, the newly formed body of the man lost its clay-like appearance and took on the appearance of a "flesh-and-blood" human body. Except for Raphael, all the angels around Randy were caught up in absolute wonder at this new creation of their King. It took Randy a few moments to realize that from their perspective, they were seeing a human being for the very first time. The more he thought about it, the stranger it felt to him to be looking upon the very body of Adam—the first man   a body that still waited to be brought to life.

"Master," Michael said, "this new creature 'man' has eyes but cannot see, ears but cannot hear, hands but cannot raise them, and feet but cannot walk."

"Yes," the King replied, "but I am not through with My creation. I shall now breathe into him a part of My eternal Spirit. As My divine breath fills his lungs, he shall become a living soul, a being with life and function. He will be a free moral agent, possessing free will—the freedom to choose. His mind shall receive some of My wisdom; it shall be an imaginative, inventive, and creative mind. He shall immediately be able to speak and carry on an intelligent conversation with us."

Randy's eyes grew wide as he watched the King place His hands on the shoulders of the man He had formed, draw him close to Himself, and breathe into his nostrils the breath of life.[21] Immediately, the man's chest expanded as his lungs filled with air. His hands began to move and his eyes opened. He took one look at his Creator, his face lit up with an expression of pure joy, and he said, "My Lord and my God, how wonderful You are!"

All the heavenly host broke out into praises, rejoicing as they shouted, "Hallelujah! We have a new addition to the great created family of God!"

Caught up in the wonder and excitement of it all, Randy found himself rejoicing along with all the others. He knew the creation story very well from reading his Bible and from teachings in his church, but to actually *see it*! He now had a whole new perspective on it. There was a beauty, a majesty, a grandeur to the whole thing that he had never fully realized.

Just then a sobering truth invaded his thoughts. Randy remembered what happened next in man's history and that memory tempered his joy. He glanced up to see Raphael looking at him with those piercing eyes and wondered if the angel could read his thoughts. "If only things would have remained this way," Randy said.

"Yes," Raphael replied. "If only."

Randy's attention was drawn once more to the scene on earth before him. The King had placed Adam in the midst of a lush and beautiful garden and was giving him instructions. As the two of them walked together in the garden, Randy noticed that Adam was indeed the "spitting image" of the King; they could have been twins. "You are My overseer for this realm," the King told Adam. "Be fruitful and increase in number; fill the earth and subdue it. Rule over the fish of the sea and the birds of the air and over every living creature that moves on the ground. The seed-bearing plants and those that bear fruit are yours for food.[22] Your responsibility is to tend this garden and keep it. You are free to eat from any tree in the garden except for the tree of the knowledge of good and evil. Eating of that tree will mean your death."[23]

The King then set Adam to his task of meaningful work. The man got busy tending the garden and giving names to all the creatures in the domain that the Creator had placed in his charge. Adam soon noticed that although all the other creatures were paired as male and female, he was alone—one-of-a-kind.

"It is not good for Adam to be alone," the King said. "I will make a helper suitable for him—a compatible companion."[24] Randy watched closely and marveled again as the King put Adam into a deep sleep, took a rib from his side, and from that rib fashioned a female compatible with Adam in every way. When Adam saw the female, he said, "This is now bone of my bones and flesh of my flesh; she shall be called 'woman,' for she was taken out of man."[25]

"Master," one of the angels asked, "are these two human beings all you need to fulfill Your will and eternal plan for their creation?"

"No," the King answered. "The man and the woman are the first of My *eternal* creatures to be endowed with the power of procreation. Through their physical union they will reproduce, bringing forth other beings like themselves. In this way they will fill the earth with human beings just as I have ordained. This power of procreation is necessary for the fulfillment of My eternal plan for creating man."

For a time Randy watched in silence as Adam and Eve went about their tasks and enjoyed their idyllic life in the garden. He watched as they tended the garden, pruning back vines and fruit trees, and as they conversed with the King in a completely natural and relaxed manner, the way friends talk to each other. It looked so wonderfully peaceful: no fear, no sickness, no worries of any kind. Randy felt a deep longing rise up in his spirit, a yearning desire to be part of such a paradise.

Before long, however, Randy sensed trouble brewing. A large serpent, shimmering and beautiful and coiled around a tree branch, had attracted Eve's attention. With a deep sense of foreboding, Randy looked up at Raphael. "That serpent...is lucifer, isn't it?"

"Yes. Lucifer has disguised his real appearance and is speaking to Eve through the serpent." Raphael's face was very somber. "It is time. Now comes the test."

Randy continued to watch the conversation between Eve and the serpent with growing dismay. He was not privileged to hear it—the scene unfolded before him as if on a great silent screen—but he did not need to. He knew exactly what was happening. "Don't do it! Don't listen to him!" Randy urged under his breath, even though he knew it was useless.

Even as he breathed those words, he saw Eve pluck a piece of fruit from a tree—the tree of the knowledge of good and evil, the very tree the King had forbidden to them. She contemplated the fruit for a moment, and then took a bite. As she chewed, she turned to Adam, who was now standing next to her, and offered the fruit to him. Adam looked at her, then at the serpent, then back at her, and finally, at the fruit she held out to him. He stared at it for a few seconds, then took it from her hand and very deliberately bit off a piece.[26]

A collective gasp of horror arose from the gathered ranks of angels as they witnessed this blatant disobedience of the King's command by His new creation, man. Randy's heart sank, even though he had known it was coming.

In the garden below, something was happening. The remainder of the fruit dropped uneaten from Adam's hand. He and Eve looked at each other and then upward toward Heaven. Expressions of sheer terror and shame filled their faces and they cowered down and rushed into the lush undergrowth to hide themselves from each other and from the searching gaze of their King and Creator.[27]

Even though he knew it would happen, Randy felt strangely deflated by Adam and Eve's defeat in the garden. Witnessing it firsthand had brought home to him the magnitude of the tragedy as never before. He couldn't help but wonder what possible purpose God had in placing the forbidden tree in the middle of such a beautiful paradise where it could become an object of temptation. Numbly, he continued to watch as the loving King confronted His newest creation.

The King kept His word with them. He banished them from the garden and began the process of physical death working in their bodies. Finally, the King summoned cherubim and assigned them to guard the entrance to the garden and to the tree of life with a flaming sword. The last Randy saw of Adam and Eve was as they reluctantly turned their backs on the garden and walked sorrowfully away, clad in animal skins that the King had provided for them to cover their nakedness and to provide protection for them in the harsh environment they would now encounter outside the garden.

"Randy." Raphael's voice interrupted Randy's brooding thoughts. Randy looked up. "Come," the tall archangel said. "You have seen what you were brought here to see. Now it is time to talk about what you have seen."

They began walking along the balustrade. "Based on what you have seen here," Raphael said, "what can you tell me about the purpose of man?"

Randy thought back for a few moments. "Well," he began, "the King said He would create man in His own image and that mankind would fill the earth."

"Very good, Randy. How would you state that as a purpose?"

A thought formed in Randy's mind, but as if from a different mind than his. "*God created man to fill the earth with the likeness of Himself.*"

"Excellent."

"I see that as a purpose, Raphael, but I don't understand *why* God wanted to do that."

"We will talk about why a little later. For now, let's make sure you recognize all the purposes. What else did you learn about the purpose of man?"

"I'm not sure; you may need to help me."

"Think back to what the King said about leaving an everlasting memorial for all generations. What would that memorial do?"

Randy puzzled it out for a few seconds, then remembered. "Love! It would prove He is a God of love!"

"Correct. Now state it as a purpose."

Once again Randy sensed a thought that originated outside himself. "*God created man to reveal His own heart and nature as Love.*"

"Good."

"But what I don't understand is *how* the creation of man reveals God as Love."

"Patience, Randy. You will understand it better the further along we go. For the moment, let's consider the third purpose for creating man. What can you tell me?"

Randy reviewed in his mind everything he had seen but to no avail. "I'm sorry, Raphael, but I can't think of anything else."

"Maybe this will help," the angel said. "Come with me." They walked to another part of the great balcony where Michael was conversing with the King. "Listen closely, Randy," Raphael said.

Michael was speaking. "My Lord, what will You do with Your man-creature now?"

"Man has failed his first test," the King answered. "He has lost his innocence. I will now test him for over 1,600 years under a dispensation of conscience and then for another 450 years under a dispensation of human government. After that time, I will call out a special man to head up a special race of people, and they will be judged according to a dispensation of promise. This will continue for 500 years. I will then give this race of people My law and have them build a tabernacle for Me. For 1,500 years I will test them under the dispensation of law."

"What then?" Michael asked.

"Then it will be necessary for Me to go down among the human race as one of them. I will send My Son to be born as a baby and take upon Himself a human body and live among men as Jesus of Nazareth, a carpenter's son. During that time, some will also recognize Him as the Son of God. After 33 years on earth, He will die on a cross for the sins of mankind in order to break the curse that Adam's sin brought upon the race. His body will be placed in a grave, but I will resurrect Him on the third day. He will return to us in Heaven, but My Spirit will go to earth to dwell in the hearts of all who have believed in My Son. This will be a dispensation of grace—known as the Age of the Church—in which all who believe in the name of My Son will be saved. Pay close attention, Michael, when that time arrives, for I will cause the full sweep

32

of My divine wisdom to be disclosed by the Church, and the Church shall bring forth My eternal purpose for man.

"Then, at a time known only to Me, I will personally send My Son back down to earth to resurrect all the righteous who have died in Him, and to change the bodies of the living saints into immortal bodies. Lucifer and all his angels will be bound in the bottomless pit for 1,000 years. I will test man for this period of time without a devil to tempt him. At the end of that time, I will loose lucifer for a while and allow him to persuade as many humans as he can to follow him. I will then make war with lucifer. Michael, you shall lead My great army of angelic beings. My Son, Jesus Christ, shall lead My great overcoming army of saints.

"Lucifer and all the rebels from both the angelic and the human races shall be cast into the Lake of Fire, which I have already prepared for them. I will then renovate the earth with My holy cleansing fire. I will make a new earth and a new atmosphere around it. I shall then place all of those humans who have qualified and met My requirements upon the new earth and they shall inhabit it forever."

Again Michael spoke. "Lord, will mankind ever again be able to communicate and fellowship with us in full visibility and reality?"

"Oh, yes. I have planned for man to be a part of My eternal family; and when My span of time is over for dealing with man, I will lift him back up, even higher than he was before he fell. At that time he shall know even as he is known. Until then, he shall know and understand only in part."

Michael and the King moved away, still talking, and Raphael turned to Randy. "Does that help? Let me give you a clue. The third purpose of man has to do with testing."

Slowly, Randy was beginning to comprehend more. "Testing involves freedom. Man could not be tested unless he was free to choose—and free to fail."

"Yes, go on."

"So man had to be created as a free moral agent so he could be tested."

"Correct. Why does man need to be tested?"

"So he can be purified and prepared to reign with Christ in eternity."

"Exactly. And Christ set the example with His life. Can you state this as a purpose?

"God created man with free moral agency so he could be tested, tried, purified, and conformed to the image of Christ in order to be prepared to reign with Him in eternity."

"Excellent, Randy."

"But how does that work? I don't understand. I'm sorry, Raphael, but I'm just eager to know."

"And you will—in time. All of these principles will require more instruction and a lot of personal reflection before you will fully comprehend them. For the time being, let's go on to the next one."

Randy was really warming up to this now. "God created man with the ability to procreate, but that is similar to the first purpose of filling the earth."

"Yes, but there is more to it than that. How did the King say His Son would go to earth?"

"He would be born as a baby. That's the Christmas story. Jesus was born of a virgin, Mary."

"And who was His father?"

"God was His father, through the Holy Spirit."

"So then, unlike Adam, whom God created directly, Jesus was God's genetic, biological son by human procreation. At the same time, Jesus was also the eternal, divine Son of God. The two go together in God's eternal purpose."

"I think I understand," Randy said. *"God created man with the power of procreation so that He could father a genetic, biological Son and not a created son like Adam.* What I *don't* understand is *why* God wanted a biological Son in the first place. What was His reason, His purpose?"

"Patience, Randy. I know you are anxious, but you need to finish laying the foundation before you can start building on it. You're doing quite well, so let's continue. The next two purposes for man have to do with the Church. What does your Bible say about the relationship between Christ and the Church?"

"Well, it says that the Church is the bride of Christ, but that it is also the body of Christ."

"Correct. Those two descriptions lie at the heart of the next two purposes. All of these purposes build on the previous one. What is the purpose of the Church?"

"To bring people into the family of God through faith in Christ."

"So the Church, the bride of Christ, is made up of many members. It is not one, but many."

"Oh, I get it!" Randy said. Once again, an outside impression had illuminated his mind, as if a silent voice was speaking into his spirit. *"God created man in order to provide a many-membered bride for His Son."*

"Right," Raphael confirmed. "Now, as the body of Christ, what is the Church to do?"

"The Church is to continue the work Christ started—to carry out the commission He gave before He ascended to Heaven. We are partners, or co-laborers, with Him in doing God's will on the earth."

"Can you state that as a purpose?"

"Let's see... How about this: *God created man in order to bring forth the Church as the body of Christ on earth to co-labor with Him as joint-heirs in carrying out God's eternal purpose.*"

"Very good."

"But *why* did God choose to do it that way? Why would He take such a risk by entrusting so much of His purpose to mankind? Why..." Randy stopped suddenly as he saw Raphael staring at him with his deep, penetrating eyes. "I know, I know...I will understand it better later. Why don't we go to the next one?"

"Don't worry, Randy, you are doing very well. Besides, the last two reasons are pretty simple. You shouldn't have any trouble with them. Before you came here and saw all of this, what would you have said was the purpose for man?"

"Well, I've always heard that we were created for worship and fellowship with God."

"Correct. See how simple that was? Now, can you state that in two purposes?"

"God created man to offer up praise and worship to Him."

"Yes; and the second?"

"God created man for fellowship with Him."

"Excellent, Randy. There you have it: eight reasons why God created man."

"All right, Raphael," Randy said, "I may have stated them, but I'm not sure that I really understand them the way I want to. As a matter of fact, I never dreamed that there was so much behind God's purposes for creating man. Besides, why did God specifically want man when He already had millions of angels? Why didn't He simply create more of you? You've hit me with so much information since I've been here that it's all becoming muddled in my brain. I simply don't understand it all."

"Understanding the purpose of man is why you are here. Now that you have stated each purpose, it's time to go back to the beginning and examine each purpose one by one in more detail."

Raphael began walking toward the far end of the balcony. "Follow me, Randy."

"Where are we going?"

"I am taking you to someone who will help you answer all your questions."

Randy fell into stride beside Raphael and the two of them walked off together as Randy, in animated excitement, fired one question after another at the tall archangel.

2

CREATED IN GOD'S IMAGE AND LIKENESS

"Who is it you are taking me to see?" Randy asked as they walked along toward the far end of the balcony.

"A man who is very wise in the Word and the ways of the Lord," Raphael replied. "A man who throughout his life has helped many people with questions like yours to understand the purposes of God."

"A man? You mean we're not going to see another angel?"

"Where humans are concerned, we angels are primarily messengers or guardians. Besides, who better than another human to help you understand God's purposes for creating the human race?"

"Well, I just thought you were supposed to explain these things to me."

"My assignment was to bring you here and get you started. I could answer all your questions, but not as fully as this man can. As a human like yourself, 'The Prophet' will be able to provide insight into the human experience that I, not being human, cannot."

As they approached the edge of the balcony, Randy noticed a small, nondescript door in the wall of the King's great palace. It was built of strong, solid wood, with iron hinges and an iron latch and bolt.

The pair stopped walking and Raphael pointed at the door. "Go through that door, Randy, and you will meet 'The Prophet.'"

Randy hesitated a few moments. "Aren't you coming with me?"

"No. You won't need me. Once you have spoken with 'The Prophet' and have learned everything you need to learn, you will come back through this same door. I will be waiting for you."

"But…"

"Don't be afraid, Randy. You'll be fine. Go on, now. He's waiting for you. Just follow the path."

Reluctantly, Randy lifted the iron latch and pulled the heavy door open. As he stepped across the threshold he cast one final look behind him. Raphael was standing there watching him, with the balcony of Heaven and the bright image of the earth in the background. Then, taking a deep breath, Randy turned around once more and stepped forward into whatever lay ahead.

The door clicked shut behind him. Immediately Randy, to his utter surprise, found himself not inside another portion of the King's palace, but on a stone path running through the middle of a grove of trees. Directly overhead, branches of the trees on either side of the path came together to form a leafy canopy that filtered the bright sunlight into a soft glow all around him.

"Where am I?" Randy whispered. "This doesn't look like Heaven." He turned around and saw that the door through which he had entered was, on this side, built not into a stone wall but into a thick, green hedge. He also noticed that the inside of the door had no latch or handle of any kind.

"How am I supposed to get back out later?" Randy asked out loud. "Hmm, I guess there really is no turning back now." Resolutely, Randy turned away from the door and began following the stone path through the grove of trees. A short distance ahead of him, the leafy canopy ended and the sunlight beyond was much brighter.

As soon as Randy stepped out into the open sunlight, he stopped and looked around in stunned amazement. His suspicion that he was no longer in Heaven was confirmed in an instant. There was no sign anywhere of the King's palace or of any other structure. Above him, the sun shone down from a blue and cloudless sky. Tree-dotted hills rolled gently to the horizon in every direction. He saw birds flying in the sky and heard them singing in the trees. The stone path on which he stood wound its way around and between the hills in front of him until it disappeared around a bend to the left some distance away.

"I guess this path leads to 'The Prophet,' whoever he is." Randy began walking again, making his way at a moderate pace along the smooth-stoned path before him. The air was clear and a little cool, like an early autumn day. It was farther to the place where the path disappeared than Randy expected. He reached it after 20 minutes of steady walking, and by that time he was sweating slightly.

Rounding the bend in the path, Randy saw immediately that a short distance ahead the path forked into two branches. When he reached the fork he stopped. "Great! Now which way do I go?" The left fork followed the hills as far as he could see until it vanished in a distant copse of trees. The right fork, on the other hand, ran for about a quarter of a mile, rising slightly to end in front of a small cottage. *That must be the place*, Randy thought. *At least, it looks more promising than the other path.* He set out again at a brisk pace along the right fork.

It took Randy only a few minutes to close the distance. The cottage was neat and trim, tan with green shutters and a slate roof. Flowers bloomed in beds on either side of the door. The stone path ran right up to the door; there were no steps and no porch. The door itself was made of solid oak with a heavy brass knocker in the center.

Randy was reaching for the knocker when the door opened of its own accord. As he looked through the doorway into a small parlor, a voice called out from the back of the cottage. "Come in, Randy. Make yourself at home. I'll be with you in a moment."

Surprised to learn that The Prophet already knew who he was, Randy stood in the doorway for a few moments longer. Finally, he stepped inside and the door clicked shut behind him. The parlor, though small, looked cozy. A couch was set against one wall with two soft chairs facing it and a brown wooden coffee table between. From the back of the cottage came the tinkling sound of ice in glasses.

Randy was still standing just inside the door, unsure of what to do, when The Prophet entered from the kitchen carrying a pitcher of tea and two ice-filled glasses on a small tray. A thick mane of white hair crowned his head. He looked straight at Randy, the sparkle in his sharp blue eyes hinting at the fire underneath. A broad smile creased his face as he said, "Welcome! Welcome! You're right on time."

His voice had a warmth and richness that to Randy seemed fitting for a man known as "The Prophet." As he set the tray down on the table, The Prophet gestured toward the couch with one hand. "Please. Sit. Get comfortable. We have a lot to talk about."

Still in a daze, Randy walked over to the couch and sat down. He simply did not know what to make of his surroundings or of the dynamic old man who sat across from him.

The Prophet held up the pitcher. "Tea?" he asked.

Randy managed to mumble out a "yes," and took the glass held out to him.

"Now," The Prophet said, settling back into his chair, "you're here to find out everything you can about why God created the human race."

Randy finally found his voice. "News travels fast. How did you know that is why I came? For that matter, how did you know my name beforehand?"

"Indeed," The Prophet replied, "news *does* travel fast, especially when you and I share the same acquaintances. I was informed beforehand both of your arrival and of your reason for coming. I have been expecting you for two days."

"Two days!" Randy exclaimed. "Two days ago *I* didn't even know I was coming!"

"Remember, Randy, in God's economy, time is always a flexible commodity."

Randy sipped at his tea and nodded. "I know. I keep forgetting that." He glanced around the room once more. "Where are we? I mean, where is this place?"

"Where do you think we are?"

"It doesn't look like Heaven. Besides, you're human aren't you? That's what Raphael told me."

"Yes, Randy. I am just as human as you are. And you are correct; this is not Heaven."

"Is it earth?"

"Let's just say it is a place set aside by the Almighty specifically for meetings such as you and I are having right now."

"You don't live here, then?"

"No," The Prophet answered. "I come whenever I am called upon."

"How do you get here?"

"Oh, the King has His ways, as you have already discovered."

Randy nodded. "He certainly does. By the way, since you know my name, how should I address you? 'The Prophet' seems so impersonal."

"My name is not important. I am simply a servant of the Lord Most High. However, if it will make you feel more comfortable, you may call me 'Eli.'"

An appropriate name for a prophet, Randy thought. "Thank you, Eli."

Eli smiled and then fixed his sharp blue eyes on Randy's face. "Well, then; shall we get started?"

"Sure." Randy set his empty tea glass on the table and settled back into the couch.

"Randy," Eli began, "tell me what you have learned so far."

"Well, Raphael and I talked about eight reasons God had for creating mankind. I think I am beginning to understand, but I still have many questions."

"Let's start at the beginning," Eli said. "State the first reason and we will go from there."

"*God created man to fill the earth with the likeness of Himself.* God created man in His own image and likeness, but what I don't understand is *why* He did it. Why was that important to God?"

"Let's see if we can find out." Eli rose from his chair, walked over to a small bookcase and withdrew two Bibles. Handing one to Randy, he sat back down with the other one. "Nothing like going straight to the source. Let's open together to Genesis chapter one. Randy, would you read verses 26-28?"

Finding the place, Randy read:

"Then God said, 'Let Us make man in Our image, according to Our likeness; let them have dominion over the fish of the sea, over the birds of the air, and over the cattle, over all the earth and over every creeping thing that creeps on the earth.' So God created man in His own image; in the image of God He created him; male and female He created them. Then God blessed them, and God said to them, 'Be fruitful and multiply; fill the earth and subdue it; have dominion over the fish of the sea, over the birds of the air, and over every living thing that moves on the earth.'"[28]

"These verses," Eli said, "reveal God's first purpose for mankind. In them we find His original mandate to us. What is the first thing we learn about man from these verses?"

"God created us in His own image and likeness."

"Yes. God *created* man. We did not evolve from a lower form of life. God created us in His own image. Notice that male and female *both* reflect the image of God. Male and female *together* comprise the race of 'Man.'"

"But what exactly does it mean to be created in the *image* and *likeness* of God? Don't those two words mean the same thing?"

"Not exactly. *Image* has to do mainly with appearance while *likeness* relates to character. In other words, *image* is physical and *likeness* is spiritual. God created us both to *look* like Him and to *be* like Him. All plants and animals on earth are alive biologically, but they do not possess an eternal spirit. That is unique to mankind. Out of all of God's creation—including the angels—only we human beings were created in His image and likeness. We alone were created to look and act like Him."

"Wait a minute," Randy said. "Doesn't the Bible say that God is a *spirit*? How can physical creatures *look like* a spiritual being?"

"You are correct, Randy," Eli replied. "Jesus said, 'God is Spirit, and those who worship Him must worship in spirit and truth.'[29] However, the Gospel of John also tells us that Christ Himself was the agent of creation: 'In the beginning was the Word, and the Word was with God, and the Word was God. He was in the beginning with God. All things were made through Him, and without Him nothing was made that was made.'[30] When Christ came to earth, He was born as a human just like us, yet He was present at creation itself. Although He took on our likeness, it was a likeness that He determined and created from the beginning—His own likeness. In that sense, we look like Him."

Randy recalled from earlier how he had seen God and Adam walking in the garden together and they had looked like twins. "I think I understand now," he said.

"Good. Let's continue. What else do these verses in Genesis say about man?"

"God commanded us to be fruitful and multiply and gave us dominion over the rest of creation."

"Yes. God's original mandate to mankind was to exercise dominion over the rest of the created order on earth. As human beings, we were created to be in charge of the physical domain—to rule with God and carry out His will and purpose in the world. That is why He gave us the power of procreation and commanded us to 'be fruitful and multiply'; in other words, to reproduce."

"But all life forms on earth reproduce," Randy pointed out. "What makes humans so special in that regard?"

"We are the only *eternal* beings endowed with that capability," Eli answered. "As far as we know from Scripture, none of the angels have procreative ability. Plants and animals reproduce and procreate, but they do not possess eternal spirits. As humans, we are spiritual beings linked to physical bodies, and God has designed us specifically for procreation. Therefore, procreation is also part of God's purpose for creating man—part of His original mandate."

Randy reflected on this for a few moments, and then nodded with growing understanding. "So God had more in mind than simply creating beings in His own image and likeness. If that was all He was after, He could have stopped with Adam and Eve. He wanted an entire race of beings that were like Himself."

"Exactly. *God's original purpose was for mankind to be a creation in God's own image and likeness who would reproduce themselves until the earth was filled with an entire race of beings in God's image and likeness.*"

"What about the Fall?" Randy asked. "Didn't Adam and Eve's sin in the garden affect God's mandate? Does it still hold true?"

Eli sat forward in his chair and looked Randy straight in the eyes. "You tell me, Randy. What do you think?"

"I'm not sure. I mean, sin destroyed or at least distorted God's image in us. What did that do to God's original purpose?"

"When was God's mandate to man given—before the Fall or after it?"

"Before."

"That's right. And God's purposes never change."

"So His original mandate still applies."

"Yes. God created us to dwell on the earth and to fill it with others of our own kind, all of whom are fashioned in the image and likeness of God, however tarnished that image may be. Genesis 5:1-3 says that God created man—male and female—in His own likeness, and that Adam, at the age of 130, begot a son in *his* own likeness and image and named him Seth. Cain and Abel, Adam and Eve's first two sons were already out of the picture. Cain murdered Abel and was banished by God to be a wanderer the rest of his life. It was a direct descendant of Seth, Noah, who built the ark and preserved eight people to carry on God's commission to man—to multiply and fill the earth. Today there are over six billion people in the world. That part of God's mandate, at least, mankind has been very faithful in carrying out."

"But as sinners we do not bear the image and likeness of God in the way He desires."

"No, we do not. That is one reason why God sent His own Son to earth. Christ came to restore God's image and likeness in mankind to its original state. God's original purpose remains the same. Mankind and the earth are linked together forever."

"You mean until we reach Heaven?"

"No, Randy, I mean *forever*. The planet Earth is mankind's eternal home. In the renewed eternal order to come, *Earth will be the 'main street' of Heaven*."

Randy sat up in surprise. "I've never heard that before!"

"Few people have. The truth is, however, that God's plan is for all of His people—all of redeemed mankind—to live forever on a renewed earth in flesh-and-bone bodies that will never die. That was His original intention for Adam and Eve in the garden. They could have lived forever in their physical bodies until they sinned against God."

"Do you mean their physical bodies were originally designed to last forever?"

"That is what most people believe. From my own studies, however, I believe that they were created with mortal physical bodies of flesh and blood and bone. As long as they obeyed God and continued to eat from the tree of life that was in the garden, they would live forever. The moment they sinned, however, their physical bodies became subject to death. One of the reasons God banished them from the garden was to prevent them from eating of the Tree of Life and living forever in their sinful, fallen state."[31]

"I understand that part of it, Eli," Randy said, "but I'm still having trouble with the concept of man and the earth being linked together forever. That's a stretch for me."

"You're not alone. I felt the same way once. If you examine it closely, however, it is really very logical. For example, we are linked to the earth first of all by creation. God not only created us *for* the earth, He created us *from* the earth."

"Oh, I see what you're getting at. God created man from the dust of the earth."

"Exactly. Let's look at Genesis 2:7-9."

After locating the passage, Randy read aloud:

"And the Lord God formed man of the dust of the ground, and breathed into his nostrils the breath of life; and man became a living being. The Lord God planted a garden eastward in Eden, and there He put the man whom He had formed. And out of the ground the Lord God made every tree grow that is pleasant to the sight and good for food. The tree of life was also in the midst of the garden, and the tree of the knowledge of good and evil."[32]

"God formed man from the dust of the ground," Eli said. "We are made up of the same stuff as the earth. Chemically, our bodies are composed of the very same elements, minerals, and compounds found in the soil: carbon, iron, potassium, oxygen, nitrogen, water, etc. Here's a question for you, Randy: What accounts for the difference? Why are we alive when the 'dust of the ground' from which we are made is not?"

"The breath of life!" Randy answered. "After forming man from the dust of the ground, God breathed the breath of life into him."

"That's right. We humans are linked with the earth by creation because we are made of the same material. The breath of God animates us and gives us life."

"I've noticed something else," Randy said. "Not only did man come from the ground, but the trees did also—including the tree of life and the tree of the knowledge of good and evil."

"Very good, Randy. In everything pertaining to life and death, we are linked intimately with the earth. Look at what God said to Adam in verses 16 and 17: 'And the Lord God commanded the man, saying, "Of every tree of the garden you may freely eat; but of the tree of the knowledge of good and evil you shall not eat, for in the day that you eat of it you shall surely die."'[33]

"In the beginning, only the tree of the knowledge of good and evil was off limits. Adam and Eve were free to partake of the tree of life as often as they wished. Once they disobeyed God, however, and reversed His order by eating of the tree of the knowledge of good and evil, they lost access to the tree of life. At that moment, their bodies began the slow process of aging and deterioration that led ultimately to their physical deaths. Every human being since then has inherited that same characteristic of physical mortality. Unless Jesus returns first, all of us who live are destined to die physically and our bodies to return to the dust from which they came. This is exactly what God told Adam when He said:

> 'Cursed is the ground for your sake; in toil you shall eat of it all the days of your life. Both thorns and thistles it shall bring forth for you, and you shall eat the herb of the field. In the sweat of your face you shall eat bread till you return to the ground, for out of it you were taken; for dust you are, and to dust you shall return.'[34]

Randy said, "I understand that our bodies return to dust when we die, but death was not part of God's original plan for man. Jesus came to do away with death and give us eternal life."

"That's right. Now let me ask you this: Is our eternal life spiritual or physical?"

"I've always heard that it was spiritual, but since you said that God's plan is for us to live on a renewed earth in flesh-and-bone bodies, I'm beginning to see that it may be both spiritual *and* physical."

"You are correct. When Jesus was raised from the dead on the third day after His crucifixion, His was a *bodily* resurrection. The Bible says that just as Jesus was raised bodily from the dead, so shall we also be raised bodily from the dead. Someday every person who has ever lived on earth will be resurrected to stand before the judgment seat of Christ. Where is Christ's body now?"

"In Heaven with God the Father?"

"Yes. Ephesians 1:20 says that Jesus is seated at God's right hand in the heavenly places. When Christ returns, He will return *bodily* to the earth and will change *our* bodies—whether we are alive or dead—into glorious bodies like His own that are not subject to disease, decay, and death. The apostle Paul said it this way: 'We also eagerly wait for the Savior, the Lord Jesus Christ, who will transform our lowly body that it may be conformed to His glorious body.'"[35]

"What about people who died without believing in Christ?"

"They will be raised also, but at a different time and in a different manner. Look at it this way: God created man originally to live forever in flesh-and-blood bodies. He also knew that if man sinned, those bodies would become subject to death. After death, those bodies would turn back into dust for a period of time, while the spirits of the people who inhabited them would go to God's designated place: either hell, for unbelievers, or paradise, for believers. However, every human body is destined to be resurrected and reunited with the spirit that inhabited that body before death. *Every* human body that has ever lived on planet earth will be resurrected.

"The righteous will live on God's cleansed heavenly new earth in their resurrected (or for those who are still alive when Jesus returns—translated) bodies which have been made immortal; incorruptible, non-dying bodies able to function eternally on heavenly new earth. On the other hand, the spirits of all of unrighteous mankind will be reunited with their resurrected bodies and cast alive into the lake of fire. There they will suffer eternal death."

"What you're saying then is that believers and unbelievers alike will be resurrected but to different destinies."

"Exactly. Let's look at some Scriptures. First, Acts 24:15. In this chapter, Paul is defending himself before the Roman governor Felix from accusations made against him by some of the Jewish religious leaders who were opposed to his message. Notice what Paul says in verse 15: 'I have hope in God...that there will be a resurrection of the dead, both of the just and the unjust.'"[36]

"Next, let's look to the Old Testament. What does Daniel 12:2 say?"

Finding the verse, Randy read: "And many of those who sleep in the dust of the earth shall awake, some to everlasting life, some to shame and everlasting contempt."[37] Randy was silent for a few seconds then said, "I see what you mean, Eli. The 'just' will be resurrected to eternal life while the 'unjust' will be resurrected to an eternal death of 'shame' and 'contempt.'"

"Yes. Both resurrections will be bodily in nature and both will involve full sensual capacity—the ability to feel and perceive with all the senses. For unbelievers, hell will be just as real a conscious and 'felt' experience of anguish and horror as Heaven will be of joy and fullness for believers. The death and resurrection of Jesus Christ makes it possible for anyone who believes to miss the first and make the second."

"But how does Christ do that? How does He make that possible for us? That's what I don't understand."

"Don't worry, Randy. No one fully understands *how* the death and resurrection of Christ accomplishes a saving work in us. That is one of the mysteries of God. What we do know is that somehow, Jesus reversed the pattern of sin that Adam began. He broke the curse on mankind. What Adam did, Christ undid. Jesus' sinless and perfect life represents what Adam was supposed to have been. Paul said it this way in Romans:

'Therefore, just as through one man sin entered the world, and death through sin, and thus death spread to all men, because all sinned... Therefore, as through one man's offense judgment came to all men, resulting in condemnation, even so through one

Man's righteous act the free gift came to all men, resulting in justification of life.'[38]

"He spoke in a similar way to the Corinthians:

'For since by man came death, by Man also came the resurrection of the dead. For as in Adam all die, even so in Christ all shall be made alive.'[39]

"The phrase 'in Christ all shall be made alive' refers to *bodily* resurrection. Adam's sin brought the curse of physical death onto the entire human race, but Christ's death and resurrection brought the certainty of resurrection to mankind's physical bodies. Jesus' death reconciled to God spiritually all who believe on Him, and His resurrection authorized and released the resurrection of every human body. Someday there will be a physical resurrection not only of believers, but of unbelievers also.

"Our bodies, then, are eternal, even though they will temporarily return to dust if we die before Christ returns. Although our bodies will die, our spirits will live on. Eventually, however, we will be reunited with our bodies that have been resurrected and restored to a state of perfection that will last forever. We are eternal. This is why Christians need not fear death. You ask me how this will work? I don't know. God does, so we'd better just leave it in His hands."

"Eli," Randy began, "there's something else that bothers me. I have heard of some preachers and Bible teachers who claim that *everybody* will be saved someday—that only satan and his angels will be in hell and that every human who has ever lived will be in Heaven."

"Yes," Eli replied with a frown. "That is a doctrine known as 'universalism.' It is based on a misinterpretation of several key Scriptures, including First Corinthians 15:22, especially the part that says, 'in Christ all shall be made alive.' Universalists interpret that as a reference to spiritual life, or salvation, but as you and I have seen, it refers to *bodily* resurrection only. The Bible contains many other Scriptures that clearly indicate that believers and unbelievers have different destinies. For example, Hebrews 9:27 says, 'It is appointed for men to die once, but after this the judgment.' What's the use of judgment if everyone will end up in the same place? What's the use of believing in Christ if it will make no difference in the end?"

Randy nodded. "I see what you mean."

"Not only that," Eli continued, "but the Book of Revelation clearly speaks of a separation between believers and unbelievers: separate resurrections and separate judgments—a complete divergence of destinies. The 20th chapter is a good example. This of course is the chapter that talks about the millennium. In the first three verses, satan is bound and thrown into a bottomless pit for 1,000 years. Let's focus on the next three verses:

> *'And I saw thrones, and they sat on them, and judgment was committed to them. Then I saw the souls of those who had been beheaded for their witness to Jesus and for the word of God, who had not worshiped the beast or his image, and had not received his mark on their foreheads or on their hands. And they lived and reigned with Christ for a thousand years. But the rest of the dead did not live again until the thousand years were finished. This is the first resurrection. Blessed and holy is he who has part in the first resurrection. Over such the second death has no power, but they shall be priests of God and of Christ, and shall reign with Him a thousand years.'*[40]

"Do you see the distinctions, Randy?" Eli asked.

"I think so. Those who remained faithful to Christ are raised to reign with Him for 1,000 years while the rest of the dead are still in their graves. This is the 'first resurrection.' Apparently, then, there are two resurrections—a first for the faithful in Christ and a second for everybody else. The reference to 'the second death' implies a *first death* as well."

"You are correct on every point. The rest of the chapter, beginning with verse 11 explains the 'second death' more clearly:

> *'Then I saw a great white throne and Him who sat on it, from whose face the earth and the heaven fled away. And there was found no place for them. And I saw the dead, small and great, standing before God, and books were opened. And another book was opened, which is the Book of Life. And the dead were judged*

according to their works, by the things which were written in the books. The sea gave up the dead who were in it, and Death and Hades delivered up the dead who were in them. And they were judged, each one according to his works. Then Death and Hades were cast into the lake of fire. This is the second death. And anyone not found written in the Book of Life was cast into the lake of fire.[41]

"This is known as the 'Great White Throne' judgment, which will occur at the end of the millennium and after the second resurrection. The 'second death' is the final judgment of unbelievers—those who died without faith in Christ—and their consignment to the lake of fire. This passage makes it clear that there *will* be human beings in hell.

"So now we have two deaths and two resurrections. Can you summarize them, Randy?"

"The *first death* is when a person dies physically, an experience that all humans share. The *first resurrection* is the bodily resurrection of the faithful in Christ alone, who are raised to reign with Him. The *second resurrection* is the bodily resurrection of all other humans who have ever lived. The *second death* is when all unbelievers are sentenced to the lake of fire. This is a final judgment that believers—the children of God—do not experience."

"Very good, Randy. What I hope you understand from all of this is that when God created man in His own image and likeness, He gave him a physical body intended to last forever. That is still His plan. Sin brought physical death and decay of the body into mankind's experience, but the death and resurrection of Jesus reversed that process. *All* human beings will one day be raised *bodily*—the unrighteous to a fully conscious eternity devoid of joy and peace and full of horror, pain, tragedy, sorrow, and separation from God in hell, and the righteous to a fully conscious eternity without pain or sorrow and filled with bliss, joy, and meaningful and fulfilling work in the constant presence of God. Do you understand?"

Randy nodded.

"Good. Why don't we take a break?"

A few minutes later, Randy and Eli were walking in a small orchard grove behind the cottage. Although the sun was high overhead, the air around them was still comfortably cool and filled with the sweet scent of apples. As they passed underneath one tree, Eli plucked two ripe apples from one of its branches. Handing one to Randy, he immediately bit into the other one. Between bites he said, "I think this is an appropriate setting to talk about what happened in the garden after God created Adam and Eve, as well as its continuing implications for mankind. After all, humanity started out with such marvelous potential: created in God's image and likeness, enjoying unbroken fellowship with God, and charged by Him to procreate and fill the earth with other humans created in His image. What went wrong?"

Chewing his own apple, Randy pondered Eli's question silently for a few moments. He was aware once more of an outside impression illuminating his mind like a silent voice speaking into his spirit. Finally, he said, "Well, first of all, Adam and Eve disobeyed God. Satan deceived Eve into eating fruit from the tree of the knowledge of good and evil. After sowing a seed of suspicion in her mind that God might be withholding something good from her, he convinced her that eating the fruit would open her eyes and make her 'like God.' Eve fell for it, ate the fruit, and then gave some to Adam, who also ate it."

"The tragic thing," Eli said, "is that Adam and Eve were *already* like God. Buying into satan's lie gained them nothing but cost them everything. What happened next?"

Randy's inner voice continued prompting him. "Satan was right; their eyes were opened, but not in the way they expected. The only 'knowledge' they gained was that they were naked and were now exposed in their sinful disobedience of God. They now knew the difference between good and evil and that they had willfully traded the good for the evil. Not only did they know *about* evil, they knew evil intimately because it was now a central part of their nature. Their sin awakened in them a moral consciousness, which they knew instantly that they had violated."

"How did God respond?"

"After confronting them with their sin, He cast them out of the garden to prevent them—as you said earlier—from eating of the tree of life and living forever in their sinful condition."

"So even their exile reflected God's love and mercy. By leaving the garden, Adam and Eve also forfeited the daily presence of God. No more open walks and talks as they had enjoyed in the garden. No more unbroken fellowship. The image and likeness of God in them were corrupted and tarnished. God's original plan seemed dead in its tracks. Nevertheless, God was determined to restore what sin had destroyed. He knew that His plan, although temporarily sidetracked, would prevail in the end. What happened to Adam and Eve after they left the garden?"

"They began having children. Cain was first, followed by Abel. One day Cain, jealous that God had accepted Abel's offering but rejected his own, murdered Abel. Some time later, Adam and Eve had many sons and daughters, but the daughters are not named. Ref. Gen. 5:4 Seth is mentioned because through his lineage, God's Son would be born. Cain and Abel took one of their sisters to be their wife. So all mankind descended from Adam and Eve.

"And with Cain's murder of Abel," Eli added, "the degeneration of mankind began. For the next 1,600 years, until the time of the great flood, God looked for someone—anyone—on earth who accurately reflected His image and likeness. In all that time He found only two. Do you remember them?"

"Yes; Enoch and Noah."

"Correct. Of Enoch the Bible says, 'And Enoch walked with God; and he was not, for God took him.'[42] Hebrews 11:5 says, "By faith Enoch was taken away so that he did not see death, 'and was not found, because God had taken him'; for before he was taken he had this testimony, that he pleased God."[43] Genesis 5:22 says that Enoch walked with God 300 years. In Enoch, God found a man who was in

His image and likeness. I believe that God took Enoch to Heaven to display to all the angelic host what man—His masterpiece creation—was to be like: Himself.

"I like to visualize it this way: For 1,600 years God looked for a man who reflected His image and likeness. About halfway through that period, He found Enoch. Pointing him out to the angels, God said, 'Watch that man Enoch. He's My kind of man; He walks like Me and talks like Me; He manifests My image and likeness.'

"They did watch—for 300 years. Finally, God said, 'I need a living model here in Heaven to put on display. Enoch, would you come up and be a living human being on eternal display so I can show all my angels what kind of man I made; show that there is still at least one who is like I want him to be? Besides, we've been walking together today and it's getting late. We're closer to My home than yours. Why don't you come home with Me?'

"Enoch did go home with God and never came back. He was translated to Heaven without dying and is still there today, on display as God's type of man. The only difference is that now Enoch has been supplanted by an even greater model of God's kind of man—Jesus Christ, God's Son."

By now, Randy and Eli had reached the back edge of the orchard, which was bordered by a white picket fence overgrown with ivy. Behind them, a few feet beyond the fence, was a small, swift-running stream. Set against the fence was an iron park-style bench, where they sat down and continued to talk.

"It seems as though Enoch was the only bright spot for God in all those generations of man," Randy said. "Until Noah, at least."

"Yes. The early chapters of Genesis paint a picture of a human race growing progressively worse until God decided to destroy them:

'Then the Lord saw that the wickedness of man was great in the earth, and that every intent of the thoughts of his heart was only evil continually. And the Lord was sorry that He had made man on the earth, and He was grieved in His heart. So the Lord said, "I will destroy man whom I have created from the face of the earth, both man and beast, creeping thing and birds of the air, for

I am sorry that I have made them"…The earth also was corrupt before God, and the earth was filled with violence. So God looked upon the earth, and indeed it was corrupt; for all flesh had corrupted their way on the earth.[44]

"Even in the midst of such corruption, however, God still looked for a model man, a man who modeled His image and likeness. He found such a man in Noah:

'But Noah found grace in the eyes of the Lord. This is the genealogy of Noah. Noah was a just man, perfect in his generations. Noah walked with God…And God said to Noah, "The end of all flesh has come before Me, for the earth is filled with violence through them; and behold, I will destroy them with the earth. Make yourself an ark of gopherwood; make rooms in the ark, and cover it inside and outside with pitch…And behold, I Myself am bringing floodwaters on the earth, to destroy from under heaven all flesh in which is the breath of life; everything that is on the earth shall die. But I will establish My covenant with you; and you shall go into the ark; you, your sons, your wife, and your sons' wives with you.'[45]

"God was so grieved in His heart over the sinful corruption of mankind that He decided to wipe them out and start over. Bible scholars have estimated that there were approximately 20 million people on earth at the time of the flood. Out of those 20 million, God found only eight—Noah, his wife, their three sons, and their sons' wives—who had remained uncorrupted.

"That's not much of a return on God's investment, is it? In a manner of speaking, you could say that God declared 'bankruptcy' and 'liquidated' His liabilities—19,999,992 of them. Then He started over with the only eight assets He had. God preserved Noah and his family in the ark as it floated on the floodwaters, which, according to the Bible, rose 20 feet above the top of the tallest mountain. After the flood, God used Noah and his family to repopulate the earth.

"I have some questions for you, Randy. Why did God go to all that trouble? Why didn't He simply destroy Adam and Eve and create a new man and woman since they failed as workable models to maintain His image and likeness? Why didn't God destroy the earth after it became corrupted and create a new one? For that matter, why didn't God take Noah to Heaven as He did Enoch instead of leaving him on earth to ride out the flood? Why cleanse the earth by water? Why not destroy it, create a new world, and start all over?"

Randy smiled as the light of insight brightened in his brain. "We've already talked about that, Eli. God has committed Himself. Mankind and the earth are linked together forever in God's eternal purpose. Since God's purpose never changes, His plan is to cleanse and renew the earth and to redeem and restore fallen man. His purpose allows for no other option. His plan *still* is to fill the earth with human beings who manifest His image and likeness."

"Excellent!" Eli returned Randy's smile, pleased at the level of his comprehension. "In order to fulfill His plan, God had to perpetuate the human race, not start over. In fact, after the flood, God gave Noah the same instruction He had given Adam in the beginning: 'God blessed Noah and his sons, and said to them: "Be fruitful and multiply, and fill the earth.'"[46]

"Even after Noah's time things were not much better with man, were they?" Randy remarked.

"That's very true, Randy. God's patience with humanity is truly beyond our understanding. He never gives up. The entire Old Testament is the story of God's determination to produce an entire race of people who are like Himself, while the very people He is trying to shape resist Him at every turn.

"The Tower of Babel is one example. Approximately 100 years after the flood, all the people of the earth were in one place, even though God had commanded them to 'fill' the earth. Instead, they decided to stay together and build a tower that would reach to Heaven, possibly with the idea of protecting themselves from being flooded out again, even though God had promised never to destroy the earth again with water. God came down, confused their language, and caused them to scatter across the face of the earth. That event gave rise to the various language groups and people groups we have in the world today.

"Around three hundred years later, God was ready to establish a nation that would be His special, chosen people. He called Abraham out of the land of Ur of the Chaldees and led him to the land of Canaan. There, God promised Abraham that all of that land would belong to him and to his descendants. Abraham had a son, Isaac, born according to the promise of God. Isaac's son Jacob, a deceiver, wrestled with God and received the name *Israel*, which means 'prince of God,' or 'he wrestled with God.' Israel had 12 sons of his own, including Joseph, from whom the 12 tribes of the nation of Israel arose.

"Famine drove Jacob and his sons to Egypt where Joseph, sold into slavery by his treacherous brothers years earlier, ruled as prime minister, second only to the pharaoh. In Egypt, Jacob's family grew into a mighty band of people, although cruelly oppressed and held in slavery by the Egyptians for approximately 400 years. At that time, God raised up Moses, who led the Israelites out of Egypt and in the wilderness of Sinai transformed this band of slaves into a nation of people chosen by God. At Mount Sinai, God appeared to His people and gave them His Law and His commandments. They built a tabernacle and worshiped Him in the wilderness. Yet even then they rebelled, and God sentenced them to wander in the wilderness for 40 years until a new generation arose. Under Joshua, that new generation conquered Canaan and established it as the homeland for God's people.

"Still the people did not follow God faithfully. After Joshua came the period of the judges, like Samson, Gideon, and Samuel, where 'everyone did what was right in his own eyes.'[47] Finally, after more than 200 years in Canaan, the people demanded a king, even though God was their king. God called out Saul as king, who proved to be a disappointment because he was a man after *man's* heart rather than God's. Next, God raised up David, whom He described as 'a man after My own heart.' David's son Solomon built the first temple for God but in his old age departed from Him to worship other gods. Solomon was a man after the world's own ideas of what it means to be successful: prosperity, get whatever you want, and live however you want. Still, God's ultimate will was not accomplished. God still did not have His ideal man."

"After Solomon, the nation split into two kingdoms: the northern kingdom of Israel and the southern kingdom of Judah. Israel, who rebelled against the house of David, corrupted themselves through repeated disobedience to God until God eventually sent them into Assyrian captivity. The northern kingdom disappeared from history. Judah was little better, their disobedience leading them into Babylonian captivity a little more than a century later. The temple in Jerusalem was destroyed. Still, God's plan for man was not fulfilled.

"During all this time, God had sent prophets to His people repeatedly in an effort to get them to repent, but to no avail. The prophet Ezekiel wrote of God: 'I sought for a man among them who would make a wall, and stand in the gap before Me on behalf of the land, that I should not destroy it; but I found no one.'[48] Isaiah wrote: '[God] saw that there was no man, and wondered that there was no intercessor; therefore His own arm brought salvation for Him; and His own righteousness, it sustained Him.'[49] This is a reference to Jesus Christ. In the end, the only way God could fulfill His plan for a race of people in His own image and likeness was to send His own Son.

"After 70 years in Babylonian exile, the Jews returned to Jerusalem and rebuilt the temple. Over the next 400 plus years, God set the stage and made the preparations for the day when His Son would come into the world."

———————

Eli fell silent and for a few minutes he and Randy sat quietly on the bench enjoying the cool afternoon breeze. Finally, Eli asked, "Are you ready to walk some more?"

"Sure," Randy replied.

They stood up and Eli led the way through a small gate in the fence. In a few moments they were walking along the bank of the stream, the rushing water providing a soft and refreshing backdrop to their conversation.

"Let's see if we can start pulling all this together," Eli began. "Randy, why did Jesus come to earth? What relationship does His coming have to God's original plan in creating mankind?"

"Jesus Christ came to earth as the 'second Adam' in order to succeed where the first Adam failed. He was the climax, the fulfillment of everything toward which God had been working ever since Adam's fall in the garden."

"The fulfillment, yes, but not the end. Jesus was the first, the 'prototype,' if you will, of a new kind of man. He came to *recreate* a new race of mankind in God's image and likeness. God's plan will not be complete until Christ has filled the earth with others of His kind. It was for this very reason that Jesus established the Church during His earthly ministry. The Church, which is called 'the Body of Christ,' is the organism through which the propagation of that new race is to come. In fact, we could refer to this new race of mankind created in Christ Jesus as the '*Church race*.' Now tell me, Randy, how did Christ accomplish this? What did it take to create this new race?"

"Well, first of all, He had to die. His death was God's judgment on our sin, making it possible for us to be forgiven. Second, He had to rise from the dead as a proof and a guarantee of eternal life."

"Good. Creating this new race required Jesus' death and resurrection or, in other words, His *blood* and His resurrection. Let's examine some Scriptures to clarify this. You said that Jesus had to rise from the dead as 'proof' of eternal life. The apostle Paul stated it this way: 'But now Christ is risen from the dead, and has become the firstfruits of those who have fallen asleep.'[50] In other words, just as you said, Christ's resurrection guarantees that all who believe in Him will also rise from the dead bodily, just as He did. As believers, our spirits are already alive forever. Someday our bodies will be raised and changed from corruptible into incorruptible—eternal bodies to house our eternal spirits.

"This 'Church race' is made up of all who profess and acknowledge Christ in faith—whether Jew or Gentile. Through His death, Christ removed the barrier separating the two to make *one* race of people in His image and likeness. Paul describes it very well in the second chapter of Ephesians. Randy, why don't you read verses 11-18."

They stopped under a large tree next to the stream while Randy found the passage. Then he read:

"Therefore remember that you, once Gentiles in the flesh—who are called Uncircumcision by what is called the Circumcision made in the flesh by hands—that at that time you were without Christ, being aliens from the commonwealth of Israel and strangers from the covenants of promise, having no hope and without God in the world. But now in Christ Jesus you who once were far off have been brought near by the blood of Christ. For He Himself is our peace, who has made both one, and has broken down the middle wall of separation, having abolished in His flesh the enmity, that is, the law of commandments contained in ordinances, so as to create in Himself one new man from the two, thus making peace, and that He might reconcile them both to God in one body through the cross, thereby putting to death the enmity. And He came and preached peace to you who were afar off and to those who were near. For through Him we both have access by one Spirit to the Father."[51]

Eli turned around and began walking back the way they had come, toward the orchard. As Randy followed, Eli asked, "Randy, according to these verses, what brings us near to God?"

"The blood of Jesus."

"And what else does Jesus' death accomplish?"

"It breaks down the wall of separation between Jew and Gentile."

"Do you understand what that means?"

"It means that whether we are Jew or Gentile, we are one in Christ. We come to Christ in the same way. His blood obliterates the difference."

"Yes. Jesus' blood makes us one—all of us who believe in His name. The word *one* occurs four times in these verses: He has made 'both one,' He has created 'one new man,' He has reconciled both to

God in 'one body,' and gives us all access to the Father through 'one Spirit.' This 'one new man' is the 'Church race,' a race of people like Jesus in spirit and behavior. In this way, Jesus fulfills God's original plan to fill the earth with people created in His own image and likeness. But how do we *become* this new creation?"

"The Bible says we have to be born again," Randy replied. "Jesus told Nicodemus, 'Unless one is born again, he cannot see the kingdom of God...Unless one is born of water and the Spirit, he cannot enter the kingdom of God. That which is born of the flesh is flesh, and that which is born of the Spirit is spirit.'"[52]

"And when we *are* born again, we become a new creation as much as when God created Adam and Eve. As Paul told the Corinthians, 'Therefore, if anyone is in Christ, he is a new creation; old things have passed away; behold, all things have become new.'[53] How do we get there? Through the blood of Jesus. Acts 20:28 says that Jesus 'purchased' the Church with 'His own blood.' Simon Peter wrote that we were redeemed not with 'corruptible things, like silver or gold...but with the precious blood of Christ.'[54] John said that 'the blood of Jesus Christ...cleanses us from all sin.'[55] Paul writes in Colossians 1:20 that Christ has 'reconcile[d] all things to [God]...whether things on earth or things in heaven, having made peace through the blood of His cross.' The blood of Jesus is key. Before we can be raised to eternal life, either bodily or spiritually, we must be cleansed of our sins by the blood of Christ.

"Continuing on in Colossians, Paul says, 'And you, who once were alienated and enemies in your mind by wicked works, yet now He has reconciled in the body of His flesh through death, to present you holy, and blameless, and above reproach in His sight.'"[56]

"Holy, blameless, and above reproach," Randy repeated. "That sounds like another way of describing the image and likeness of God."

"Excellent observation, Randy. Those words accurately describe Adam and Eve the way they were before the Fall—and the way we will be in the life to come, thanks to Jesus. After all, that is why He came: to recreate a new mankind in God's image and likeness. And He does it by changing us one by one, one life at a time.

"No matter what we may go through in life as a Christian, we can rest assured that God is fulfilling His purpose to fashion us in His own image and likeness. Paul expressed it this way in Romans: 'And we know that all things work together for good to those who love God, to those who are the called according to His purpose. For whom He foreknew, He also predestined to be conformed to the image of His Son, that He might be the firstborn among many brethren.'[57] *Predestined* means that God established it beforehand. God's purpose, determined before the foundation of the world, was that we would be 'conformed to the image of His Son.'

"Jesus Christ is the prototype, the first living example, the first reality of the new creation that's going to fill the earth and fulfill the original mandate of Adam and Eve to multiply, fill the earth with Godlike creatures that are in His image and likeness. And God is determined to mold, shape, and conform us to that same image. Another way of describing what it means to be created in the image of Christ is found in Ephesians 2:10: 'For we are His workmanship, created in Christ Jesus for good works, which God prepared beforehand that we should walk in them.'

"We are destined to be conformed to the image and likeness of Christ, who is Himself the very image and likeness of God, His Father. Jesus authorized this by His resurrection. *Jesus was—and is—God's perfect man in the image and likeness of God. Through His death and resurrection, Jesus became God's redemptive sacrifice for man—man's perfect God.*"

"I have one other question, Eli. *How* is Christ conforming us to His image, at least while we are still in *this* life?"

"Good question. After Jesus was resurrected He divided His ministry of building His Church into five gifts. These gifts were given for the purpose of equipping members in the gifts of the Holy Spirit and to help them be transformed into Christ's image and likeness. Paul describes this very well in the fourth chapter of Ephesians when he says:

'And He Himself gave some to be apostles, some prophets, some evangelists, and some pastors and teachers, for the equipping of the saints for the work of ministry, for the edifying of the body of

Christ, till we all come to the unity of the faith and of the knowledge of the Son of God, to a perfect man, to the measure of the stature of the fullness of Christ; [and,]...speaking the truth in love, may grow up in all things into Him who is the head—Christ—from whom the whole body, joined and knit together by what every joint supplies, according to the effective working by which every part does its share, causes growth of the body for the edifying of itself in love.[58]

"Jesus gave Himself to the Church as the five gifts of apostle, prophet, evangelist, pastor, and teacher to equip and perfect His new creation until they come to the place of being without spot or blemish, united and perfected into the fullness of the image and likeness of Christ, who is God's standard for His new creation, the 'Church race' of mankind. Perfected and conformed in Christ's image and likeness, we will fill God's new earth and rule and reign over it forever, just as He planned from the beginning."

"Wow!" Randy said, shaking his head. "That's quite a plan!"

"Isn't it?" Eli smiled. He opened the gate and they walked back into the orchard. The sun had dropped low into the western sky. "I think we've covered enough for now," Eli continued. "There's a room in the cottage all made up and ready for you. Why don't you relax and make yourself at home, and we'll take this up again tomorrow."

"Sounds great!" Randy replied as they walked back to the cottage together.

3

CREATED TO REVEAL GOD'S LOVE

Before sunrise the following morning, Randy woke to the smell of sausage cooking. He lay quietly in the small bed for a few minutes, savoring the aroma, and watched the sun come up through the east-facing window. It looked to be another beautiful day. Randy wondered if there was ever anything other than beautiful days here. He still did not know exactly where "here" was. Eli's explanation yesterday had contained more than a hint of mystery.

He got out of bed and stood by the window. The rolling terrain with its grassy hills and groves of evergreen trees looked earthlike enough, yet different somehow. Everything before him seemed fresh and new, almost pristine, as if untouched and uncorrupted by the hand and civilization of man. "I wonder if this is how the world looked when it was new," he thought. He paused for a moment longer, then prayed, "Thank You, Lord, for the beauty of this day and of this place. Help me today to understand what You have sent me here to learn."

Then Randy walked into the kitchen where Eli was just serving up two plates of scrambled eggs, sausage, and toast.

"Good morning, Randy," Eli said in a bright voice. "How did you sleep?"

"Like the proverbial log. The best night's sleep I've had in months."

Eli nodded. "That's what this place does for you. There is a peace—a serenity—here that I can explain only as the peace of God. It seems to surround and permeate everything. It's as though while here all the cares and fears of normal life are suspended, or even banished."

They sat down at the table and Eli took a moment to bless the food.

As they began eating, Randy asked, "Can you tell me any more about where we are, exactly?"

"No more than I told you yesterday. I really don't know myself. All I can say is that this is a place the King has prepared—whether on earth or somewhere else, I don't know—for times of retreat and repose and for learning the answers to inquiries such as yours."

Between forkfuls of egg Randy said, "I've been thinking about it and, even though this is not really a garden, it seems in many ways like what I imagine Eden was like."

"You noticed that, did you," Eli said with a smile as they continued to eat.

———

Soon after breakfast, Eli and Randy were seated in the parlor where they had begun the day before. Birds twittered softly in the tree outside the window. A gentle breeze wafted through the room, bringing with it the sweet scent of honeysuckle. Sunk well back into the soft couch, Randy felt like he could stay here forever. It was Eli who got things rolling.

"Well, Randy, yesterday we covered the first purpose for God creating man: *to fill the earth with beings created in His own image and likeness.* Do you have any further questions about that purpose?"

"No, I think I'm pretty clear on that one."

"Fine, then let's move on to the next one. What is the second purpose you want to discuss?"

"God created man to reveal His own heart and nature as Love."

"All right. To start off with, what questions do you have?"

"Just one, mainly. I know and understand that God loves us. What I don't understand is how God's creation of man *reveals* His love. How is the creation of man an *expression* of God's love nature?"

"That's a good question, Randy. Let me ask you this: What is the *greatest* expression of God's love for us?"

"Sending Jesus Christ, His Son, to die on the cross for our sins."

"Correct. Now, keeping that truth in mind, let's go back to your original question: How does the creation of man express God's nature of love? I think the best way to approach it is to do a comparison between man's perspective and God's perspective. First, let's look at the benefits that *man* receives from Jesus' death on the cross and, second, the benefits that *God* receives from the death of His Son. In the process, I think the relationship between the creation of man and God's love nature will become clear.

"To begin with, what is the greatest benefit mankind received from Jesus' death on the cross?"

"For all who trust Him, salvation—the forgiveness of our sins and a right relationship with God."

"And who established the standards that define that right relationship and how to obtain it?"

"God did."

"Exactly. As the Creator of man, God is the only one who has the authority and the right to establish the means by which man could have atonement, forgiveness, and cleansing of his sins. In other words, once mankind fell into sin, our relationship with God was broken. When Adam and Eve were cast out of the garden of Eden, they were cast out of God's presence. Sin separated us from God; a barrier we could not remove. God was the only one who could establish a means of reconciliation. If we were ever to get rid of our sins, be forgiven, and be reconciled with God, God Himself would have to establish the way. Fortunately for all of us, He did.

"Randy, do you remember the first thing Adam and Eve did after they ate the fruit from the forbidden tree of the knowledge of good and evil?"

"Well, the Bible says that their eyes were opened and they realized that they were naked, so they sewed fig leaves together to cover their bodies."

"That's right. And a little later, God improved on that first effort. Genesis 3:21 says, 'Also for Adam and his wife the Lord God made tunics of skin, and clothed them.' Why tunics of skin?"

"Because they would last longer than fig leaves and would be better suited for the harsher environment outside the garden."

"Both of those are true, but covering their physical nakedness was not really the central issue here. Why did God clothe them with tunics of *skin*?"

"Oh, I think I see where you are going with this," Randy said. "This is the first example of a blood sacrifice to atone for sin."

"Exactly. God killed an innocent animal—probably a lamb or a goat—and clothed Adam and Eve with its skin. Even at this early stage, the shedding of innocent blood as a sacrifice to atone for sin was established by God as the means by which man could be reconciled to Him. There is no other way. Hebrews 9:22 says that without the shedding of blood, there is no remission of sins.

"Adam and Eve tried to cover their guilt by their own efforts but God showed them that His way—the shedding of innocent blood—was the only acceptable way. Of course, Jesus eventually made the ultimate sacrifice for sin. The shedding of His sinless blood made atonement and forgiveness possible for all people. Every animal sacrifice prior to Jesus' death pointed to His death, even this very first sacrifice on the threshold of Eden.

"We find this principle of the blood sacrifice reaffirmed in the very next chapter in the contrasting ways God responds to the offerings of Cain and Abel. Let's look at Genesis 4:2-7."

Quickly locating the passage, Randy read:

"Now Abel was a keeper of sheep, but Cain was a tiller of the ground. And in the process of time it came to pass that Cain brought an offering of the fruit of the ground to the Lord. Abel also brought of the firstborn of his flock and of their fat. And the Lord respected Abel and his offering, but He did not respect Cain and his offering. And Cain was very angry, and his countenance fell. So the Lord said to Cain, 'Why are you angry? And why has your countenance fallen? If you do well, will you not be accepted? And if you do not do well, sin lies at the door. And its desire is for you, but you should rule over it.'"[59]

"Have you ever wondered why God accepted Abel's offering but not Cain's?" Eli asked.

Randy thought for a moment then replied, "I heard a preacher say once that Cain's offering was rejected because it was produce from the ground, which God had cursed."

"That's true; Genesis 3:17 says that God did curse the ground on account of Adam's sin, but that is not why He rejected Cain's offering. There is another reason."

Randy's eyes lit up in understanding. "Blood! Cain's offering was not a blood sacrifice. That's why God rejected it!"

"Correct. Abel's offering was of 'the firstborn of his flock and of their fat.' The reference to 'fat' means he killed his offering. He shed its blood and God received it as an acceptable offering. Cain brought an offering of vegetables, which God rejected because it was not a blood sacrifice."

"It seems also as though God was just as concerned about Cain's attitude as he was the nature of his offering. After all, God said to Cain, 'If you do well, will you not be accepted?'"

"An excellent observation, Randy. God is always interested more in what we are than in what we do. Sin always begins as a desire or an attitude before it shows up as an action. Although the Bible does not tell us, it is reasonable to believe that through the years Adam offered blood sacrifices to God in the manner that God had shown him and that he taught his sons to do the same. Like his parents before him, Cain tried to do things his own way. He brought a rebellious offering to God because his spirit was already in rebellion. God confronted Cain in hopes that he would repent, but he didn't."

"And Abel died because of it."

"Yes, unfortunately. God is no respecter of persons but He does look for a faithful heart. He accepts obedience but rejects disobedience. He accepts His way but rejects our way. Cain had the opportunity to obey and be accepted, but chose to remain in rebellion and murdered his brother out of jealousy."

Randy said, "I had always thought that the system of animal sacrifices began with Moses and the Israelites after they left Egypt."

"That is when God codified the practice in the Law and set down specific procedures for it, but blood sacrifice was quite common before then. Noah did it, and so did Abraham and Jacob."

"But animal sacrifices can't really take away sin can they? I mean, that's why Jesus had to die, isn't it? Only His death could cleanse our sin."

"You are correct, Randy. The blood of animals could not cleanse man from sin. Animal sacrifices only served to postpone God's wrath against sin and point to the day when the ultimate sacrifice, the Lamb of God, would take away sin once and for all. Turn to Hebrews chapter 10 and read verses 8-14."

Randy read:

"Previously saying, 'Sacrifice and offering, burnt offerings, and offerings for sin You did not desire, nor had pleasure in them' (which are offered according to the law), then He said, 'Behold, I have come to do Your will, O God.' He takes away the first that He may establish the second. By that will we have been sanctified through the offering of the body of Jesus Christ once for all. And every priest stands ministering daily and offering repeatedly the same sacrifices, which can never take away sins. But this Man, after He had offered one sacrifice for sins forever, sat down at the right hand of God, from that time waiting till His enemies are made His footstool. For by one offering He has perfected forever those who are being sanctified." [60]

"The beginning of this passage quotes from Psalm 40. Considering the entire context, who is speaking the words, 'Behold, I come to do Your will, O God'?"

"Jesus?"

"That's right. What do the words, 'He takes away the first that He may establish the second' refer to?"

"The 'first' refers to the system of animal sacrifices, and the 'second,' to Jesus' sacrificial death on the cross."

"Yes; very good. Jesus came to do away with the old covenant of animal sacrifices and replace it with the new covenant based on His own once-for-all sacrifice as the Lamb of God who takes away the sin of the world. Two things are explicit in this passage. First, the animal sacrifices that the priests offered 'repeatedly' could *never* take away sins. Second, Jesus' death was a *one-time* sacrifice for sin that takes it away forever: He offered His body 'once for all'; He 'offered one sacrifice for sins forever'; by 'one offering' He 'perfected forever those who are being sanctified.'

"In other words, what thousands of animal sacrifices could not do, Jesus did by offering up His own body once-for-all. Sacrificial animals had to be perfect and without blemish, foreshadowing the sinless perfection of the One who would one day shed His own blood for the sin of mankind. Jesus, having died once and been raised from the dead, is now seated at the right hand of God, waiting for the day when all things in Heaven and earth finally will be delivered to Him.

"Here's another question for you: Why did it have to be Jesus? Why couldn't God have chosen someone else—Enoch, say, or Noah, or one of the other righteous people in the Bible—to atone for the sins of mankind?"

Randy smiled. "That's easy, Eli. No matter how righteous any of those people were, as descendants of Adam they still were contaminated with the stain of the sin nature. They could not atone for the sins of mankind because they had sins of their own, just as we all do. Even their best was not sufficient, and neither is ours. It had to be Jesus because, of all human beings who have ever lived, He alone was without sin. Only someone without sin could be the pure and acceptable sacrifice for sin."

Eli nodded in satisfaction. "Excellent, Randy. That is also why it is true that salvation is found only in Christ. Only in Him can we find forgiveness. Only in His blood can we be cleansed of sin. By God's design and plan, faith in Christ as Savior and Lord is the *only* way for us to be reconciled with God. Scriptures supporting this are abundant. First John 1:7 says that the blood of Jesus cleanses us from all sin. Verse 9 says that when we confess our sin, He is faithful 'to forgive us our sins and to cleanse us from all unrighteousness.'

"First John 2:2 says, 'And He Himself is the propitiation for our sins, and not for ours only but also for the whole world.' Do you know what *propitiation* means?"

"Doesn't it have something to do with turning away God's anger over our sin?"

"That's close. Propitiation means satisfying God's holy and righteous requirement for the judgment of sin. As the 'propitiation for our sins,' Jesus, by His death, satisfies God's requirement that our sin be judged. God placed our sins on Jesus at the cross and judged them there so that we could be forgiven and receive eternal life.

"Propitiation means that Jesus took our place. God Himself planned it this way. Paul said that we are 'justified freely by His grace through the redemption that is in Christ Jesus, whom God set forth as a propitiation by His blood, through faith, to demonstrate His righteousness.'[61] This demonstrates God's love for us: 'In this is love, not that we loved God, but that He loved us and sent His Son to be the propitiation for our sins.'[62]

"A couple of other Scriptures make it clear as well that Jesus is the only way to be reconciled with God. First Timothy 2:5 says: 'For there is one God and one Mediator between God and men, the Man Christ Jesus.' Speaking of Jesus, Peter said: 'Nor is there salvation in any other, for there is no other name under heaven given among men by which we must be saved.'[63]

"Let's try to pull this together now. What was the significance for mankind of Jesus' birth, death, and resurrection? What benefits did mankind receive from Jesus Christ coming into the world?"

"The forgiveness of our sins—a way to be reconciled with God."

"Good. And how does that relate to God's original plan for creating man?"

"By being reconciled to God, we are restored to the place of being able to fulfill God's original purpose for us—to fill the earth with a race of beings like Himself."

"That's right. You've summed it up very well, Randy. I think we are now ready to turn the page and talk about the benefits God received by sending His Son into the world and how the creation of man demonstrates God's essential nature as Love."

———•·•———

After a short break, Eli and Randy resumed their discussion in the parlor of the small cottage. It was moving toward noon. A soft breeze, warmer from the advancing sun but still comfortable, blew through the window. Eli had set a plate of crackers and cheese and a pitcher of lemonade on the table between them.

Between bites of cheese and sips of lemonade, Randy spoke first. "Eli, before we go on, I do have one question about God's purpose in sending Christ to earth to die for our sins."

"Yes, Randy?"

"Over the years I have heard several preachers preach on this subject in a way that left the impression that Christ's mission on earth to save mankind was an afterthought with God. They seemed to suggest that the Fall of man in the garden of Eden somehow took God by surprise and He had to come up with a way to reconcile lost humanity back to Himself—a 'Plan B' so to speak. My problem is that this goes against my understanding of God. I would think that *nothing* ever takes God by surprise."

"How right you are, Randy," Eli replied. "Nothing surprises God. Nevertheless, many Christians labor under the false impression you mentioned. Whether due to poor preaching or teaching or to simple misunderstanding, they assume that God developed His plan for man's salvation *after* the Fall. That is *totally* incorrect. The Scriptures bear out the fact that Jesus Christ was slain in the mind and purpose of God not only before the human race came into being, but even before the foundation of the world. Let's look at a few examples. First, Matthew 25:34."

Randy read: "Then the King will say to those on His right hand, 'Come, you blessed of My Father, inherit the kingdom prepared for you from the foundation of the world.'"

"Good. Now, Matthew 13:34-35."

"All these things Jesus spoke to the multitude in parables; and without a parable He did not speak to them, that it might be fulfilled which was spoken by the prophet, saying: 'I will open My mouth in parables; I will utter things kept secret from the foundation of the world.'"

"Ephesians 1:4."

"Just as He chose us in Him before the foundation of the world, that we should be holy and without blame before Him in love."

"Okay. First Peter 1:20."

"He indeed was foreordained before the foundation of the world, but was manifest in these last times for you."

"And finally, Revelation 13:8."

"All who dwell on the earth will worship him, whose names have not been written in the Book of Life of the Lamb slain from the foundation of the world."

"All right, Randy, tell me: What phrase is common to each of those verses?"

"The phrase 'the foundation of the world.'"

"Correct. The Greek word for 'foundation' is *katabole*, which means 'a casting or laying down; founding.' In other words, Christ's death on the cross was established in the mind and plan of God from before the very conception or founding of the world. It definitely was *not* an afterthought with God. He created the original, beautifully arranged earth and everything on it with the death of His Son for the sins of mankind in mind."

"Thanks, Eli. That really helps clarify the issue for me."

"It's good that you brought it up, because it leads very naturally into the next phase of our discussion: What did God get from the death of His Son on the cross? What purpose did Calvary fulfill for God? What personal desire of His did Calvary meet? How does the creation of man reveal God's nature as Love? What possible purpose could God have for creating a whole race of beings that He knew would end up costing the death of His Son to redeem them?"

"I've really been puzzling over that idea, Eli," Randy said. "I understand why God was determined to redeem mankind rather than start all over: we are linked to the earth forever and God committed Himself to that plan at the very beginning. My problem is this: Why did God decide to create man in the first place if He knew we were going to sin and cause all these problems for Him and make it necessary for Him to sacrifice His own Son to bring us back?"

"The answer to that question lies at the very center of God's nature, the inner core of His being. We see the expression of that purpose in Jesus' death and we have already touched on it."

"Jesus' death demonstrates God's love for us."

"Yes. Here's the answer in a nutshell. God redeemed us through the blood of Christ because He loves us, but He created us *in order to love us*! Jesus' death on the cross gave God the opportunity to demonstrate to all creation His core nature, eternal being, and the motivating purpose behind all that He does, which is *love*.

"Tell me, Randy, besides the death of Jesus, how do we know God loves us?"

"The Bible tells us, just as in the song I learned years ago, 'Jesus loves me this I know, for the Bible tells me so.'"

"The Bible does indeed reveal many things about God, and His love for us is certainly one of them. God's Word is progressive revelation, meaning that God reveals Himself a little bit at a time. The further we go in the Bible, the more about God we learn. From which part of the Bible does most of our knowledge of God's love come—the Old Testament or the New?"

"Isn't His love taught throughout the Bible?"

"Yes, of course it is, but as progressive revelation, the entire Old Testament sets the stage for one event."

"The coming of Christ!"

"Right. And Christ's coming, with His subsequent death on the cross and resurrection from the dead, is the ultimate expression of God's love found in the Scripture."

"I see what you're getting at," Randy said. "God's love is revealed throughout the Bible but most completely in the New Testament with the Gospel stories of Jesus Christ."

"Yes. And Paul's letters and the other Epistles expand on that theme. If we did not have the New Testament, we could still know that God loved us because of Old Testament Scriptures that say so, but the *love* of God is not revealed in the Old Testament to the same extent as some of God's other characteristics."

"What do you mean?"

"The Old Testament reveals three major attributes of God: His *omnipotence*, His *omniscience*, and His *omnipresence*. Are you familiar with those terms, Randy?"

"I've heard of them. Omnipotence means that God is all-powerful; omniscience, that He is all-knowing; and omnipresence, that He is present everywhere at once."

"Very good. Yes, the Old Testament reveals first of all that God is *omnipotent*. This means that He has unlimited power. The creation

CREATED TO REVEAL GOD'S LOVE

of the endless universe with its myriad galaxies, stars, solar systems, and planets, is a living example of God's omnipotence. The universe and all it contains reveals the omnipotent power of the One who created it all.

"Our solar system lies 28,000 light years from the center of the Milky Way galaxy, which itself is 80,000 light years across and is part of a cluster of galaxies known as the Local Group. The Local Group is part of a local supercluster that includes many clusters. Super-clusters are separated by very large voids of space with very few galaxies in between.[64] There are an estimated 50 billion galaxies in the universe.[65]

"The earth revolves around a star named Sol, which we gener-ally call the 'sun,' one of over 100 billion stars in the Milky Way. At 865,000 miles in diameter, our sun is large enough to contain 1.3 million planets the size of the earth,[66] yet it is only a moderate-sized star compared to others in the galaxy. The 'supergiant' star Betel-geuse, for example, which is 650 light years away, has a diameter the size of the orbit of Mars.[67]

"The universe is so large that man has never yet found the end of it, yet even the visible part is so vast that it would take billions of years for light to cross from one side to the other. Such vastness is beyond human comprehension, yet God created it all. *That is omnipotence!*"

Randy nodded slowly, lost in wonder trying to visualize it. Then he said, "In my astronomy class we have talked about some of these things. Everybody acknowledges the incomprehensibility of the uni-verse by any kind of human scale, yet most of them, and especially the professor, chalks it all up to 'random processes.' A Creator God fits nowhere into their picture."

"Well," Eli replied, "that just demonstrates the fact that great intellectual knowledge does not preclude spiritual blindness. A person must have spiritual eyes to perceive spiritual truth."

Randy nodded again.

"Speaking of knowledge," Eli continued, "that brings us to the second major attribute of God revealed in the Old Testament: God's *omniscience.* As you said, Randy, omniscience means all-knowing. One who is omniscient has unlimited knowledge in all things. The wisdom required to set up the laws for the rotation of the earth and for its relation to the solar system, to set the solar system in rotation in the galaxy, and the galaxy itself in rotation: all of these provide powerful demonstrations of God's omniscience. The law of gravity, the laws of thermodynamics, the design and intricate workings of the human body, especially the power of procreation, all reveal that God is infinite in His knowledge and wisdom.

"God, in His omniscience, holds the universe together. Our planet Earth, for example, is located exactly where it needs to be in order to support life. A change in the earth's orbit of only one or two degrees in either direction with relation to the sun would make life impossible. If our sun was closer to the center of the galaxy, stellar density and radiation would be too great to support life. If it was farther away, the quantity of heavy elements would be insufficient for rocky planets to form. Again, life would be impossible.[68]

"Science has discovered the 'strong nuclear force coupling constant' that holds together the particles in the nucleus of an atom. If that force was just a little weaker, multi-proton nuclei would not hold together, and hydrogen would be the only element in the universe. On the other hand, if the nuclear force was only slightly stronger, nuclear particles would bond together more firmly and more frequently. Hydrogen would be rare and the supply of life-essential elements heavier than iron, which are formed by splitting very heavy elements, would be insufficient. In either case, life could not exist.[69]

"All these things that man is only now discovering, God has known all along. He created them and set them in place just the way they are to carry out His plan and design. *That is omniscience.*"

"I've heard of some of those, and others," Randy said. "They're called 'anthropic principles,' principles or conditions that must be in place in order for life to exist. If any parameter is off by even the tiniest degree, life cannot survive. Anthropic principles are used to identify evidence of design in the universe."

"And design in the universe is evidence of God's omniscience. Very good, Randy. Not only is God omnipotent and omniscient, He is also *omnipresent.* Omnipresence is a quality of God and God *alone.* Only He can be everywhere at once. God is big enough to fill the entire endless universe, yet small enough to inhabit an atom. God's ability to be in all His endless universe at the same time, and to have everything in His sight and under His control at all times is a living demonstration of His omnipresence. He is the life-giving air we breathe as well as the light of the world and of every creature, whether on earth or in heaven.

"God not only fills all space, but all eternity as well. He has no beginning or end. With God there is no past, present, or future, but only one eternal '*now.*' The Psalmist said, 'Where can I go from Your Spirit? Or where can I flee from Your presence? If I ascend into heaven, You are there; if I make my bed in hell, behold, You are there. If I take the wings of the morning, and dwell in the uttermost parts of the sea, even there Your hand shall lead me, and Your right hand shall hold me.'"[70]

"God certainly is an incredible and awesome God," Randy said. "He is all-powerful, all-knowing, and all-present, but these attributes make Him seem distant somehow, so infinitely far above and beyond us that we could never touch Him. It's hard to see His love nature in these characteristics."

"That's quite true, Randy," Eli replied. "These characteristics show us that God is powerful in His acts, eternal in His presence, and all-knowing in His wisdom and understanding. But all these things give little opportunity for a revelation of God's inward motivating power and character—His love, in other words. To understand God's love nature most fully, we need to look at what the New Testament reveals about Him. The Old Testament talks about the love of God for His people, particularly in the Psalms and the prophets, but the New Testament is where His love is most fully revealed. Let's go to the Scriptures. First, look at John 3:16."

Randy read: "For God so loved the world that He gave His only begotten Son, that whoever believes in Him should not perish but have everlasting life."

"Now, John 15:13."

"Greater love has no one than this, than to lay down one's life for his friends."

"Okay, go to First John 3:16."

"By this we know love, because He laid down His life for us. And we also ought to lay down our lives for the brethren."

"Next, Romans 5:8."

"But God demonstrates His own love toward us, in that while we were still sinners, Christ died for us."

"Finally, First John 4:16."

"And we have known and believed the love that God has for us. God is love, and he who abides in love abides in God, and God in him."

"These are only a few of the many New Testament Scriptures that attest not only to God's love but to His essential nature *as* love," Eli said. "Do you see the progression of idea and revelation here, Randy?"

"Yes, I think so. God's love sent Jesus to earth to die for our sins. Jesus' death was proof and demonstration of that love, which is the greatest love of all. In the last verse, John explicitly states that 'God is love.'"

"That's right. And the key to how the creation of man reveals God's nature as love is also found in these verses."

"How so?"

"As you said, the last verse spells out that God is love. Aside from their reference to love, what else do the first four verses have in common?"

Randy reviewed the verses for a few moments, then said, "They all mention the death of Christ."

"Correct. That's the key. *God created the human race in order to bring about Calvary—Christ's death on the cross.* By so doing, He revealed His essential nature of love."

Randy shook his head, confused. "I still don't follow you."

"We've already talked about how Jesus' death on the cross was the greatest demonstration of God's love. The Son of God—God incarnate, God *in the flesh*—died to redeem His own people. Because God is a Spirit, He cannot die. In order to show His love by dying for us, He had to have a *physical body*, a *mortal* body that *could* die. Before He could have a mortal body, He had to have a race of beings who had mortal bodies, beings like Himself in image and likeness, a race He could be born into as one of them and die for their redemption."

Randy's eyes widened in understanding and he nodded. "Okay, I think I'm beginning to see. God created the human race so He would have a means of obtaining a body for Himself so that He could die for the sins of that race, and so demonstrate His love."

"Exactly. God created the human race to bring about Calvary—the cross—so that He could demonstrate His core nature—love—that defines who He is and motivates everything He does."

"Still, Eli, why did God have to create *man* to show His love? Why couldn't He show His love to the angels that He had already created?"

"Because of the nature of His love. The love of God, or *agape* in the Greek, is by nature a self-giving love. Agape love cannot be fully demonstrated by the giving of *things*. Agape love can be demonstrated fully only by the giving of oneself. Therefore, agape love is sacrificial in nature. The greatest demonstration of sacrificial love is when one person gives his life for another. That is why Jesus said, 'Greater love has no one than this, than to lay down one's life for his friends.'[71]

"Another reason God could not demonstrate agape love to the angels has to do with reciprocity. For agape love to be complete and fulfilled, it must be shared with someone who can reciprocate; someone who can return that love in like kind. Only someone who is like the giver can return the same kind of love. In other words, God could fully demonstrate and express His nature of agape love only to beings who were like Himself. The angels, although they are spiritual beings, are not like God because they were not created in His image and likeness. Out of all God's creations, only man is created in His image and likeness. We alone are like Him, so it is only to us that He can fully express His nature of agape love. He created us in order to do just that.

"Until He created the human race, God had no way to demonstrate His core being of love. Jesus demonstrated the love of God to the ultimate degree by giving Himself in death on the cross for the redemption of fallen mankind. Calvary was a demonstration to all of creation that *God is love*. For mankind this was not only a revelation, but redemptive."

"I guess that's why God couldn't die for the fallen angels, too," Randy said.

"Partly. There are a couple of other reasons as well why God did not die for the fallen angels. First of all, from all we can tell from the Scriptures, fallen angels are not redeemable. Apparently, God has no plan of redemption for spirit beings who sin. This means that when lucifer and his angels rebelled against God they were lost forever. God's redemptive plan applies only to beings who have mortal bodies.

"Secondly, God is a Spirit and *cannot* die. Before He could show His love by dying, He had to have a mortal, flesh-and-blood body that *could* die. Before He could get that body, He had to create a race of beings who had mortal bodies. In order for His love to be fully expressed, those beings with mortal bodies had to be like Him. God, who cannot die, created man, creatures like Himself in image and likeness, but with mortal bodies that can suffer, bleed, and die. He endowed them with procreative power so they could fill the earth with others like themselves and so that, in due time, He could take on a body of flesh like theirs and demonstrate His agape love nature by dying for their sins.

"All of this was fulfilled with the coming of Christ. When Jesus was born of the virgin Mary, He was God incarnate—God in the flesh. Speaking of Jesus, Hebrews 10:5 says, 'Therefore, when He came into the world, He said: "Sacrifice and offering You did not desire, but a body You have prepared for Me."' Jesus Christ had a mortal body that bled and died on the cross. Let's look at one final Scripture that I think will tie all of this together: Hebrews 2:5-10."

Randy quickly found the passage and read:

"For He has not put the world to come, of which we speak, in subjection to angels. But one testified in a certain place, saying: 'What is man that You are mindful of him, Or the son of man that You take care of him? You have made him a little lower than the angels; You have crowned him with glory and honor, and set him over the works of Your hands. You have put all things in subjection under his feet.' For in that He put all in subjection under him, He left nothing that is not put under him. But now we do not yet see all things put under him. But we see Jesus, who was made a little lower than the angels, for the suffering of death crowned with glory and honor, that He, by the grace of God, might taste death for everyone. For it was fitting for Him, for whom are all things and by whom are all things, in bringing many sons to glory, to make the captain of their salvation perfect through sufferings."[72]

"What does it mean to say that Jesus was 'made a little lower than the angels'?" Eli asked.

"That means He was born a human being and took on a human body."

"Correct. One thing that makes mankind unique from the angels is that we have a physical, mortal body while the angels are spiritual beings only. We are lower than the angels in the sense that our mortal bodies can die, while angels, as spirits, never die. The day will come, however, when we will be given renewed bodies that will never die, and in that day we will no longer be 'lower than the angels.'

"According to these verses," Eli continued, "why was Jesus 'made a little lower than the angels'?"

"So that He could suffer death and taste death for everyone."

"And what would His death accomplish?"

"Through His death, Jesus would bring 'many sons to glory.'"

"What does that mean, Randy?"

"It means that through Jesus' death, all humans who believe in Him are redeemed, forgiven of their sins, and restored to the full image and likeness of God and to their original place in God's plan."

"Very good. Let's see if we can wrap this up now. What is the second purpose for God creating man?"

"God created man to reveal His own heart and nature as Love."

"And why was the creation of man necessary in order for God to reveal His agape love nature?"

"God needed a mortal body that could suffer, bleed, and die because agape love cannot be fully expressed except by giving itself sacrificially for another. God created the human race—body, soul, and spirit—with a mortal body that could suffer, bleed, and die, so that He could demonstrate His love by dying for mankind to redeem us from our sins."

"Excellent, Randy! Do you have any other questions?"

"No, I'm fine," Randy said.

"Good. Then let's break for lunch."

4

CREATED AS A FREE MORAL AGENT

"Let's pick up where we left off," Eli said after lunch. He and Randy were seated on the bench at the back of the small apple orchard. Apple scent was in the air and the chuckling sound of the stream behind them filled their ears. "First, however, let's do a quick review. Tell me the first reason we discussed why God created man."

"God created man to fill the earth with a family of beings created in His own image and likeness," Randy replied. "Even though man fell into sin, God sent Jesus Christ, His own Son, as the 'second Adam' to restore man to his original place in God's plan. He accomplished this through His death and resurrection, guaranteeing eternal life to all who believe in Him."

"Good summary. And the second reason?"

"God created man in order to reveal His essential nature as Love. Since agape love is a self-sacrificial love, it cannot be fully expressed unless it gives itself. Since God is a Spirit being and cannot die, He needed a flesh-and-blood body that He could inhabit and use to demonstrate His love by dying for the sins of mankind. He created man with a mortal physical body so that He could do just that. Jesus Christ was God in the flesh, who willingly gave His life on the cross so that we could be forgiven and restored and receive eternal life."

"Excellent, Randy. I think we are ready to move on. What is the third reason why God created man?"

"God created man with free moral agency so he could be tested, tried, purified, and conformed to the image of Christ in order to be prepared to reign with Him in eternity."

"All right; that's an important one. I suppose you have some questions?"

"A few. I've been thinking about this one a little bit. First of all, *why* did God create us as free moral agents with the freedom to choose if He knew we would choose to sin? I mean, why did He bother? Man's freedom of choice has proven to be nothing but trouble for God. Why didn't He preprogram us to always do what He wanted? You know, push a button and we'd worship, push another and we'd work. That way we'd never make mistakes. Finally, what's the relationship between being a free moral agent and being tested, and how do these things prepare us for reigning with Christ?"

Eli raised his eyebrows. "You really *do* have some questions! That's good; it shows that you are really seeking to understand these things. Part of the answer to free moral agency goes back to the first two reasons we talked about. First, man was created in God's image and likeness. God Himself is a free moral agent. As sovereign God, He does what He pleases, accountable to no one. To be created fully in God's image, man had to be a free moral agent as well; that's part of being like God.

"Second, as a God of love, God desired man to love Him in return. True love and obedience are possible only in an environment of free choice. Preprogrammed 'robots' could never truly love or obey God. We must *choose* to do these things. Only then do they become real. And in order to choose, we must have freedom of choice. In other words, we must be free moral agents.

"These are quick answers, but there is much more to this question of free moral agency."

"But are we really, truly free to choose?" Randy asked. "In my philosophy class and elsewhere I've heard discussions claiming that humanity really has no freedom of choice. We are part of a closed, deterministic system, and all our 'choices' are really predetermined, either by genetics or by some biological mechanism we don't understand yet."

"That is the basic point of view of the philosophy known as 'naturalism,'" Eli answered, "but it is not the point of view of the Bible. God did not create a closed, deterministic system. If He had, He would never 'interfere' in its workings. Miracles and other manifestations of the supernatural would not exist. Make no mistake about it, Randy, as humans we *are* free moral agents. We *do* have freedom of choice. This is clear from the earliest pages of Scripture. Let me ask you: What is the first task that God assigned Adam?"

"To keep and care for the garden."

"Yes, but God did not specify *how* that was to be done. Apparently, Adam was *free* to do it in his own time and way and however he saw fit. What was the next responsibility God gave to him?"

"God told Adam to name all the animals."

"Right. This too is evidence of free choice. Adam *chose* names for the animals and whatever name he chose for an animal, that became its name. Adam was exercising free will in fulfilling his created role as administrator of the earthly domain. We see Adam's free moral agency also in relation to Eve."

"How so?"

"The Bible says that God made Eve and brought her to Adam. God did not *force* Adam to take her. Sure, Eve was the only creature on earth compatible with Adam; the only other one like him. It was perfectly natural for Adam to accept her, but still he *chose* her. God did not force the issue."

Randy nodded. "It does seem pretty obvious then that man's free moral agency was operative even before the Fall, from the earliest days in the garden."

"Yes. Free moral agency is an essential part of human nature. It is the way God created us. Unfortunately, the clearest example of it is found in Genesis chapter three in Adam and Eve's *choice* to disobey God."

"Was that really a choice?" Randy asked. "I mean, wasn't Eve deceived by lucifer?"

"Yes, she was, but she still *chose* to disobey God. First of all, she *chose* to listen to lucifer's words even when he started saying things that went against what she knew of God and what God had said. She *chose* to follow her own desires rather than remain true to God's will. Eve's choice was influenced by lucifer's deception, but it was still a choice. Adam, on the other hand, apparently made his choice with his eyes wide open. There is no mention of deception in his case. Read Genesis 3:6."

Randy read: "So when the woman saw that the tree was good for food, that it was pleasant to the eyes, and a tree desirable to make one wise, she took of its fruit and ate. She also gave to her husband with her, and he ate."[73]

"Do you see what I mean, Randy? Lucifer enticed Eve with the three basic lusts of humanity: the lust of the flesh (the tree was 'good for food'), the lust of the eyes (the tree was 'pleasant to the eyes'), and the pride of life (the tree was 'desirable to make one wise'). His tactics never changed. The devil still tempts us the same way.

"Eve may have been deceived, but that did not excuse her from the consequences of her actions. In the end she acted according to what she *saw*. In other words, she acted *on her own*. Adam was with her and apparently made no attempt to intervene. Even worse, when she handed him the fruit, he ate it with no hesitation. Deception was involved, yes, but that did not excuse them from responsibility for their own choices. They could have chosen not to listen to lucifer, and they could have chosen to remain obedient to God. They did neither and mankind has suffered the consequences ever since."

"That brings up another question. Why did God put the tree of the knowledge of good and evil in the garden and then place it off limits? Surely He knew the object of temptation it would become."

"Indeed He did, Randy, and that's precisely the point. Free moral agency means nothing without being tested."

"Tested? What do you mean?"

"Everything in that original garden of Eden setting was established by God deliberately for the purpose of testing Adam and Eve with regard to their free moral agency. For example, earth was the age-old headquarters for lucifer and his angelic assistants as they presided over that part of the galaxy under God's appointment. After lucifer's rebellion, earth became his prison. God created man as a free moral agent and deliberately placed him on the earth where lucifer the tempter would have access to him.

"Next, God placed two trees in the center of the garden: the tree of life and the tree of the knowledge of good and evil. The fruit of the tree of life was free for the taking, but the fruit of the tree of the knowledge of good and evil was forbidden. Of that tree, God told Adam, 'you shall not eat, for in the day that you eat of it you shall surely die.'[74] From what the Scriptures tell us, God placed no other restrictions on them. Except for that one limitation, Adam and Eve were completely free to do as they pleased in the liberty of the pure and innocent nature with which they had been created.

"Did God know what He was doing? Absolutely. Although we may not always understand His ways, God has a reason for everything He does. God's reason in this case was to test the free moral agency of the human couple He had created. Even though in His omniscience God knew Adam and Eve would fail the test, the test was absolutely necessary for His eternal plan regarding man."

"Why, Eli?" Randy asked. "That's what I don't understand. Why was such a test necessary and why was it so important to God's plan?"

"Because testing is necessary to build character and develop maturity. Let me ask you this: What was the original state or condition of Adam and Eve in the garden? What kind of nature did they have?"

"They had a righteous nature, like God, because they were created in His image."

"That's what many people believe but that is not completely accurate. Adam and Eve were created in God's image, yes, but they were not created in perfect righteousness—no one is. However, they *were* created with a *pure* nature and innocent of any good or evil, yet with free moral will. It would be premature to say they were 'righteous,' because their nature and character had not yet been tested. None of us are born with fully developed character, either good or bad, and Adam and Eve were no different. Character has to be developed. Its strength comes only as it is proved and tested by being confronted with a choice to do either good or evil, to obey God or to disobey Him.

"God's plan for man required that he be tested—given a choice—so he would have the opportunity either to prove his faithfulness in being obedient to God or to reveal his unfaithfulness and rebellious heart through disobedience. That is why God put the tree of the knowledge of good and evil in the garden and placed it off limits to Adam and Eve. It was His way of testing them."

"The tree of the knowledge of good and evil is one thing," Randy said, "but what about lucifer? It seems to me that he was part of the test, too."

"An astute observation, Randy. Many people have a problem with the idea that lucifer in his evil and corrupt state could be the tool or instrument of a holy and righteous God. Keep in mind, however, that God deliberately put man on the earth within the devil's reach. God is omnipotent. Lucifer, despite his rebellion, ultimately has no choice but to serve the purposes of God. He began as a tempter in the garden of Eden and has been filling that role ever since."

Randy said, "After Adam and Eve sinned, God expelled them from the garden. The tree of the knowledge of good and evil was no longer available as a source of temptation. Where does our temptation come from now?"

"As I said, lucifer continued as man's tempter outside the garden, but to be perfectly honest, he gets blamed for many things he is not responsible for."

"What do you mean?"

"I mean that even though the devil is constantly around to tempt us, there is a second and even more powerful source of temptation for mankind—our own sinful, fallen nature."

"More powerful than the devil?"

"Oh, yes. The Bible calls our fallen lower nature the 'flesh.' After man's exile from the garden, the flesh became—and remains—the primary source of man's choices all the days of his life on earth. Romans 8:8 says that those who are in the flesh cannot please God. We can't live in the flesh *and* live in the Spirit. Bitter water and sweet water cannot come from the same fountain. That's why the Christian life consists of a constant choice between the flesh and the spirit. Those who are without Christ have only the flesh, which is why they remain in spiritual bondage to the devil; they really have no choice.

"On the other hand, we who are Christians, because we have the Spirit of God living in us, *do* have a choice. Every day we *can* choose between flesh and spirit—between ignoring God and going our own way or obeying God. The vast majority of the problems we experience in life are the result of our own fleshly choices and have nothing to do with the devil."

"What you're saying then is that throughout our lives we all have two sources of temptation, or testing of our free moral agency: the devil, who tempts us from without, and our own fallen nature, which tempts us from within."

"Exactly."

"But I thought the Bible says that God does not tempt us."

"That's right; God never tempts us in the sense of enticing us to sin. He does test us, however, for the purpose of building our character, bringing us to maturity, and preparing us for leadership in His eternal kingdom. We learn and grow through our successes as well as our failures. Often, in fact, failure is our best teacher.

"One of the ways God tests us is by *allowing* us to be tempted. But with that, it is important to remember the promise of First Corinthians 10:13: 'No temptation has overtaken you except such as is common to man; but God is faithful, who will not allow you to be tempted beyond what you are able, but with the temptation will also make the way of escape, that you may be able to bear it.' There stands the contrast: The devil tempts us out of a desire to destroy us; God tests us out of the desire to strengthen us, build our character, and shape us into overcomers, people who are equipped, prepared, and ready to rule with Him in His eternal kingdom. God is determined to make us into the people He originally intended us to be. Testing is an inescapable part of that process."

"So until Adam and Eve were tested in the garden, it was uncertain which way they would go. They were free to choose either path."

"Yes, Randy, they were free to choose. Their choice, however, was not uncertain to God. In His omniscience, God knew that they would fall. That is why He already had in place a plan to redeem fallen man through the death of His Son.

"At first, Adam and Eve were in what we could call a 'probation' period. Do you know what probation is?"

"It's a trial period, like when you start a new job. You're on probation for a certain period of time to see whether or not you can do the job."

"Precisely. Another way to define it is to say that probation is the subjection of an individual to a period of testing and trial to ascertain fitness for a job or position. Just as human employers do this for new employees, God does it for us. His purpose is to make us ready for the greater assignments and responsibilities He wants to give us. He wants us to succeed so He tests us to build in us the skills, experience, and character to do so.

"By placing us on probation, God is ascertaining whether or not we are qualified to rule and reign with Him. As free moral agents, we can choose to obey or not to obey, as well as choose how much shaping we will allow Him to do in our lives. By so doing, we are helping to determine the degree and level of responsibility and leadership we will have in His kingdom. There will never ever be anybody in a ruling, reigning class in eternity who has not been purged and purified of anything and everything that is un-Christlike or in any way contrary to God's nature, character, government, laws, wisdom, or ways.

That's why our testing in this life is so important; it prepares us for our work in the life to come. It makes us fit to rule and reign with Christ.

"One of the best definitions of this divine probation I've ever found was written by Emery H. Bancroft. It impressed me so much that I memorized it:

> 'The purpose of the probation of our first parents was, so to speak, to test their virtue—to transform their holy natures into holy characters. Moral character is produced only by probation, by the free personal choice of good in the presence of evil and with full power to choose evil or good. Now Adam and Eve were created with holy, moral natures. However, their wrong choice— that is, disobedience to God's command—transformed their holy, moral natures into sinful moral characters, and involved both themselves and their posterity in the guilt of sin and the defilement of depravity.'"[75]

"Does this mean I should look on every problem or difficulty or challenge in my life as a test from God? Sometimes those trials really hurt."

"They certainly do. And yes, regarding the trials of life as tests from God is a biblical and healthy perspective. For one thing, it helps us get the focus of our attention off the problem itself and onto the One who can carry us through it. God does not send every test that comes our way but He can use every test to fulfill His purpose to build our character and mature our faith. How much benefit we derive from our tests depends on how willing we are to embrace them as God's means of preparing us for His purposes. We can either grouse and complain as we go through the pain or we can look to God and say, 'Lord, show me what You are trying to teach me through this trial. Use it to shape me for Your will and purpose.'

"God's testing of His people is one of the major themes of the Bible. Our tests become easier to bear when we understand God's purpose behind them and that He loves us and allows us to be tested for our own good. Let's look at some Scriptures that back this up. First, James 1:2-5."

Randy found the verses and read:

"My brethren, count it all joy when you fall into various trials, knowing that the testing of your faith produces patience. But let patience have its perfect work, that you may be perfect and complete, lacking nothing. If any of you lacks wisdom, let him ask of God, who gives to all liberally and without reproach, and it will be given to him."[76]

"According to James, what benefits come from trials and testing?"

"Patience, perfection, completeness, and wisdom. In this sense, doesn't 'perfect' mean 'mature'?"

"Indeed it does. If we allow them to, trials and tests will bring us to maturity or completeness in the image and likeness of Christ, which is what God desires."

"How can we be *joyful* in trials? They're no fun at all."

"It all depends on your attitude and how serious you are about being conformed to the image of Christ. Committed athletes train incessantly, not because it is fun but because they see the end goal they are striving for. They regard the end result as worth the pain in getting there. Remember, 'no pain, no gain.' We need to learn to view our tests not as enemies or things to be feared, but as opportunities for growth. The Phillips translation of these verses says:

'When all kinds of trials and temptations crowd into your lives, my brothers, don't resent them as intruders, but welcome them as friends! Realise that they come to test your faith and to produce in you the quality of endurance. But let the process go on until that endurance is fully developed, and you will find you have become men of mature character, with the right sort of independence. And if, in the process, any of you does not know how to meet any particular problem he has only to ask God—who gives generously to all men without making them feel foolish or guilty—and he may be quite sure that the necessary wisdom will be given him.'[77]

"In other words, learn to view trials and tests not as enemies but as friends—the means a loving Father uses to bring you to maturity.

All such trials and tests are our friends. Remember Paul's words: 'And we know that all things work together for good to those who love God, to those who are the called according to His purpose. For whom He foreknew, He also predestined to be conformed to the image of His Son.'"[78]

"Paul took a similar view to James regarding trials. Look at Second Corinthians 4:15-17."

Randy read:

"For all things are for your sakes, that grace, having spread through the many, may cause thanksgiving to abound to the glory of God. Therefore we do not lose heart. Even though our outward man is perishing, yet the inward man is being renewed day by day. For our light affliction, which is but for a moment, is working for us a far more exceeding and eternal weight of glory.[79]

"Remember that for us, 'glory' means being conformed to the image of Christ. Compared to eternity and the glory and destiny that await us there, our trials and tests here on earth are nothing more than 'light affliction' that God uses to renew our 'inward man' day by day. It's all a matter of perspective.

"Throughout the Bible, trials and tests are linked to spiritual growth. Look at Psalm 34:19."

Again, Randy read: "Many are the afflictions of the righteous, but the Lord delivers him out of them all."

"And Psalm 119:67 and 71."

"Before I was afflicted I went astray, but now I keep Your word...It is good for me that I have been afflicted, that I may learn Your statutes."

"Now, Romans 8:28-29."

"And we know that all things work together for good to those who love God, to those who are the called according to His purpose. For whom He foreknew, He also predestined to be

conformed to the image of His Son, that He might be the first-born among many brethren."

"Tell me, Randy, what do all of these verses say about the role of tests in our lives?"

"Tests or afflictions serve to help us grow in faith. Somehow, they serve God's purposes."

"Very good. God does not send tests or allow temptation to no purpose. God has a purpose for everything He does. His primary concern is molding us into the image of His Son, and allowing us to endure times of testing is a major part of that process.

"Here's another question: Besides Jesus, which person in the Bible is most associated with affliction and suffering?"

"That's easy," Randy replied. "Job."

"What do you remember of Job's story?"

"Well, Job was a righteous man who feared God and served Him faithfully. God allowed satan to test Job's faithfulness through heavy suffering. Within a very short period of time Job lost his wealth, his health, and his family. He kept crying out to God and maintained his faith and integrity even when his friends tried to convince him that he must have sinned for God to afflict him so much. In the end, Job's faith held out and God restored to him twice as much as what he had lost."

"That's right. Job kept crying out for understanding of why he was suffering so. In the early chapters of the Book of Job, he is focused on himself and his affliction. Once God speaks, however, very late in the book, Job gets a whole new perspective. Although God never explains to Job the reason for his suffering, Job learns to see his life from the bigger picture of God's viewpoint. Job learns that God's ways are always perfect and that He does all things well and right, and he is content with that.

"God put more honor (and trust) on Job than on any other person in the Bible. Why? Because of Job's faithfulness. Job proved that he could be trusted with the Lord's confidence. That is why God was willing to place His reputation on the line. God said to satan, 'Have you considered My servant Job, that there is none like him on the earth, a blameless and upright man, one who fears God and shuns evil?'[80] When satan challenged God's assessment and claimed that Job served God only for what he could get out of it, God allowed satan to test Job by taking away everything he had. God knew that Job could stand up to the test because he already demonstrated his faithfulness. In the end, Job's afflictions only strengthened his faith.

"God seeks the same results in us from the tests that come our way. He wants to strengthen our faith and prepare us for leadership in His kingdom. God tests all His children; everyone who loves Him and follows Him. No one is exempt. Consider Abraham, for example. Abraham is one of the greatest figures in the Bible, yet he is also one of the most tested figures in the Bible. Abraham went through seven major tests as God shaped him for his purpose of becoming the father of the nation of Israel. The seventh and final test was the toughest of all: God commanded Abraham to sacrifice his son Isaac."

"I remember the story," Randy interjected. "God told Abraham to offer Isaac as a burnt sacrifice, and Abraham obeyed. Just before Abraham plunged the knife into his son's body, God stopped him and provided a ram to sacrifice in Isaac's place. That's when Abraham learned that God was testing his faith."

"Yes. Abraham passed the test and God said to him, 'Do not lay your hand on the lad, or do anything to him; for *now I know* that you fear God, since you have not withheld your son, your only son, from Me.'[81] Abraham was ready for his role in God's plan. God knew that if Abraham could be trusted to give up his own son, he could be trusted with anything. Abraham's test proved his fitness and maturity, not only to God, who in His omniscience already knew, but to Abraham himself. That's another purpose of testing: to build up our confidence as we meet those tests successfully. But we must always remember that our confidence is to be in God and not in ourselves."

"So God has a redemptive purpose in testing us?" Randy asked. "Even when it hurts it is for our ultimate benefit?"

"Absolutely. Just as our human parents, out of their love for us, discipline and punish us when we are wrong in order to teach us to do right, so God does as a loving heavenly Father to His children. The writer of Hebrews perhaps sums it up best:

> 'And you have forgotten the exhortation which speaks to you as to sons: "My son, do not despise the chastening of the Lord, nor be discouraged when you are rebuked by Him; for whom the Lord loves He chastens, and scourges every son whom He receives." If you endure chastening, God deals with you as with sons; for what son is there whom a father does not chasten? But if you are without chastening, of which all have become partakers, then you are illegitimate and not sons. Furthermore, we have had human fathers who corrected us, and we paid them respect. Shall we not much more readily be in subjection to the Father of spirits and live? For they indeed for a few days chastened us as seemed best to them, but He for our profit, that we may be partakers of His holiness. Now no chastening seems to be joyful for the present, but painful; nevertheless, afterward it yields the peaceable fruit of righteousness to those who have been trained by it.'[82]

"Our trials and tests, or what the writer calls 'chastening,' are signs of our sonship as children of God. If we are His children, He will chasten and discipline us 'for our profit, that we may become partakers of His holiness.' In other words, He chastens us to make us like Him—to mold us into the image of Christ. It may be painful for a while, but the end result is the 'peaceable fruit of righteousness.'"

"Eli," Randy said, "I think I understand now the importance of tests and trials in God's plan for us, but I still don't understand specifically how tests prepare us for reigning with Christ."

"Tests try our lives like fire tries gold or silver. Just as fire refines and purifies precious metals, tests, trials, and afflictions refine and purify our lives. They 'burn away' the waste, the useless, the ungodly—all the 'chaff' in our lives.

"Gold is purified by fire in levels of degrees. The hotter the flame, the purer the gold. A fire of 2,500 degrees is necessary to refine 18-carat gold. Absolutely pure gold is transparent. How hot a fire would it take to produce that? Gold cannot be destroyed by fire; fire only improves its quality.

"We are the same way. If we allow God to have His way in our lives, the trials and tests that we go through will make us better. They will strengthen our faith, purify our hearts, and sharpen our perspective so that we can focus on the things that are truly important without getting sidetracked by peripheral issues. All selfish, erroneous, and ungodly thoughts and passions will be purged from us so that when we enter eternity, we will be equipped to reign with Christ, willing to obey Him in all things.

"Such purification is necessary; every believer must go through the process. Paul told the Corinthians:

'For no other foundation can anyone lay than that which is laid, which is Jesus Christ. Now if anyone builds on this foundation with gold, silver, precious stones, wood, hay, straw, each one's work will become clear; for the Day will declare it, because it will be revealed by fire; and the fire will test each one's work, of what sort it is. If anyone's work which he has built on it endures, he will receive a reward. If anyone's work is burned, he will suffer loss; but he himself will be saved, yet so as through fire.'[83]

"Our work in life is going to be tested by the fire of God's trials. If our work passes the fire test, God promises that we will receive a reward of Christlikeness and rule and reign with Him. How well we handle our trials here will determine the degree of our reward and responsibility in eternity."

"In that case," Randy said, "our entire Christian life is one long test."

"Indeed it is. God applies His refining fire to our lives gradually, on 'low heat' at first. As we learn and grow and show ourselves faithful at that level, He cranks up the heat to prove and purify us even more. The more we grow the more 'heat' He applies, always with the goal of bringing us to the place where our hearts and spirits are as pure as the purest gold.

"Our nature as free moral agents is very important here. We cannot always choose the trials we face, but we can always choose how to respond to them, and our choice has eternal implications. Those who choose God's way, truth, and principles of living and ruling are destined to become God's kind of man—the mankind God intended from the very beginning—a mankind conformed to the image of Christ. This elected and perfected group will be privileged to co-reign with Christ as His bride on the new earth. As heirs of God and joint-heirs with Christ, they will fulfill God's original plan for mankind."

"What will that type of 'man' be like?" Randy asked. "It is hard to imagine."

"Yes, it is. Let's see if we can create a picture. First of all, God's type of man will be absolutely convinced that God is always right and His ways are always best. God is not going to risk another 'lucifer episode,' so there will be no one in the ruling and reigning class in eternity who is not absolutely convinced that God's laws and God's government are absolutely right, perfect, and just in every way at all times and in all circumstances.

"Christians who argue with God a lot show that they are spiritually immature. God calls them and they argue; He tells them to do something and they balk. Instead of obeying, they try to debate with God. As long as believers have that kind of attitude, they will not experience much victory. Nor will they experience much of the presence or power of God in their lives."

"I guess that explains part of my own problem," Randy admitted. "I know I have argued with God before."

"We all do at one time or another, Randy. It's a product of our sin nature. One sure sign of our spiritual growth is if we find ourselves arguing with God less often and obeying Him more often. Don't worry yourself too much over this. Don't focus on your failure; just focus on the Lord and on His Word and your tendency to argue with God will diminish. You're certainly not alone.

"Probably 90 percent of Christians are not completely convinced with deep inner conviction that God's ways are absolutely right and that He is just in all His doings. Most of us still have at least a glimmer of doubt in our hearts, and that is enough to trip us up. God wants to purge even that glimmer out of us and He uses the fiery trials of life to do it. When our world falls apart and our ways prove useless after all, we find ourselves in the place of having to trust God. That is when we see most clearly that His way is not only the best way, but the only way. Ninety-five percent of our temptation would be removed if we only fully believed that God's ways are right and best for our good.

"Here's another characteristic. God's kind of man will live not by outward law of do's and don'ts but by an inward heart conviction that God's ways are best. The Pharisees in Jesus' day lived by outward law but had no inner heart conviction. That is why Jesus said that if we are to enter the kingdom of heaven, our righteousness must exceed that of the Pharisees.

"God's kind of man will also be convinced that God's government, Church membership, and Church government are *forever*. The Church is eternal. It will not end with the end of this present world, but will go on forever. That means also that Church government is eternal. No one knows exactly what form that government will take, other than the fact that Christ will be the head. There will probably be some form of leadership structure of pastors, elders, deacons, helpers, servers, etc. Each believer here on earth has been given spiritual gifts, and those gifts are eternal; they will still be used in Heaven."

"How can all of this be if our free will remains completely intact?" Randy asked. "It seems as though man has been so corrupted by sin that such free submission to God in everything would be impossible."

"Impossible in our own strength, yes," Eli replied. "But don't forget that as Christians we have the Holy Spirit living in us to teach us, equip us, and help us not only to do the will of God, but to desire His will above all else. This is not a suppression of our free will but liberation of it, because it is only in the will of God that we are truly free. God created us with free moral agency, and that freedom flourishes when we choose righteousness, when we freely choose the way of the Lord. The Holy Spirit enables us to make that choice.

"Consider Jesus, for example. Jesus certainly exercised free will, yet the entire motivation of His life was to please His Father, to be like Him, to obey His will and to fulfill His Father's purpose for His life and time as a mortal man on earth. Jesus said, 'My Father has been working until now, and I have been working…Most assuredly, I say to you, the Son can do nothing of Himself, but what He sees the Father do; for whatever He does, the Son also does in like manner.'[84] Jesus' will was so surrendered to that of His Father that He said, 'the Son *can do nothing of Himself,*' yet Jesus did not obey His Father as a robot with no choice, but freely, out of love and from a desire to please His Father.

"The apostle Paul is another example. He went from a passionate persecutor of the Church to a passionate servant of Christ. Passion is impossible without free will. Paul's greatest passion was to identify with Christ's death, and to be conformed to His image. He told the Philippians that his foremost desire was 'that I may know Him and the power of His resurrection, and the fellowship of His sufferings, being conformed to His death, if, by any means, I may attain to the resurrection from the dead.'[85] Paul chose this path freely, and we see in his life a demonstration of the kind of man God desires to build in each of us.

"God has planned from the beginning to have a race of beings who will give Him 100 percent allegiance, not because of force or fear but because they are convinced that God is perfect, and that His laws, principles, and way of living for mankind are not only the right way, but the only way that is best and workable for the human race. God's eternal purpose has always been to have a race of mankind creation that willingly love, respect, and honor Him. They willingly lay down their lives and allow everything within them to be transformed into God's Word, will, and way. These humans will be one with Jesus as He is one with His Father; for that reason they will be allowed to sit down with Jesus in the heavenly places, ruling and reigning with Him over God's vast universal domain."

"So then, our free will remains fully intact, but we must allow God to mold and shape it—and us—so that we are equipped and ready to reign with Jesus, and the trials and tests of life serve that purpose?"

"Exactly. The will of all free creatures must be tested to see if they are willing to cooperate with God for the greatest good of all. Moral agents must prove themselves true by such tests and thus become worthy of the confidence of the Creator before being entrusted with the eternal administration of the universe.

"All free moral agents must have their wills purged of all possibility of falling, so there can be mutual confidence in each other. In this way there would be no possibility, on the part of man, of marring God's plans sometime in eternity through the misuse of man's will.

"Our free will must be put through all possible tests so that there can be no possible transgression against any part of the eternal plan at any time. This is the only sure way that the plan can have a guarantee of success forever."

"That sounds like a difficult process," Randy remarked. "What specifically are we supposed to learn from these tests?"

"It is a difficult process," Eli replied. "That's why we spend a lifetime learning. Essentially, we must learn and freely surrender our will to these truths:

1. *God must be respected and obeyed.* Why? Because His ways are best.

2. *His laws are final and just.*

3. *Sin does not pay and will never be excused.*

4. *God's form of government is the only correct one.*

5. *A loving and free submission to God is the highest and most noble principle of free moral government.*

6. *Justice and righteousness must prevail or no society can be eternally preserved in the universe.*

7. *Consecration to the greatest good of all is the highest good and nature of all God's creation.* There has to be a way throughout eternity to love one another, to bless one another, to serve one another, to give because God is giving. The greatest joy of Heaven is not walking down the streets of gold, or

examining the universe, or even worshiping Jesus alone. The greatest joy of Heaven will be blessing others.

8. *God is the only absolutely just and perfect being and the only one capable and worthy of unquestionable authority.* Not lucifer, not Buddha, not Mohammed, nor any other created being, but God alone.

9. *All ideas and accusations of present rebels against God are untrue.* God's truth is the only truth, and all truth is God's truth.

10. *God's way of life as revealed in His Bible is the only true way to live.* Jesus is the Way, the Truth, and the Life, and there is no other.

11. *God should, by virtue of His own position as Creator, preserver, governor, and Lordship and Redeemer, and His own history of justice and righteousness in all of His dealings, be recognized by all as the supreme moral governor of the universe.*

"Until we as free moral agents learn these lessons, we will not be fully prepared or qualified to rule and reign over any of God's kingdom whether in Heaven or on earth. However, God *will* have a 'called-out' group of humans who will meet all of these qualifications; people who will not only talk about them, but learn them and practice them in their own lives."

Randy thoughtfully considered these words for a few moments. "Eli, is this available to *any* believer? Can any one of us attain to this level, or is it reserved for a special few?"

"It is available to any believer who is willing to pay the price in trials and testing and in self-surrender. Not every believer will be willing to pay that price."

"What about you, Eli?"

Eli smiled. "I cannot say how things *will* be at that time, Randy. All I can do is tell you what my desire is—what goal I am striving for. It is the same goal that Paul had when he said, 'forgetting those things which are behind and reaching forward to those things which are ahead, I press toward the goal for the prize of the upward call of God in Christ Jesus.'[86]

"When I stand before God, I want to hear Him say to me, 'You did everything I wanted you to do. You fulfilled all your potential and accomplished everything I ever intended for you to do, plus a few extras. You went the second and the third mile.' I want to hear Him say to me the six most important words I could ever hear: 'Well done, good and faithful servant.'"

Randy nodded in agreement. "After all, what greater exercise of free will could there be than to *choose* to become everything God wants me to be—everything He created me to be. Why settle for anything less?"

"I couldn't agree more," Eli said as they stood up and walked back to the cottage.

5

CREATED SO THAT GOD COULD FATHER HIS OWN BIOLOGICAL SON

As Randy and Eli made their way through the orchard, Randy noticed that the ground beneath his feet was becoming mushy. He stopped and looked down in wide-eyed wonder as water seeped up through the soil and spread across the surface of the ground. A mist quickly formed and covered the land like a fog about six inches above the earth. As far as Randy could see, it looked as though they were walking on a cloud.

Randy looked over to see Eli eyeing him with an amused expression. "What's happening, Eli?"

Eli's eyes twinkled. "I was hoping you would get to see this while you were here."

"What is it?"

"This is how the orchard, and all the land around here, receives irrigation. You see, Randy, it *never rains here.*"

"It *never* rains?" Randy looked in astonishment at the vibrant orchard and the lush, green fields and forests beyond. "How does everything stay so green?"

"Just as you are seeing now, a mist rises up from below the earth to water the ground. This usually happens a couple of times a week. Does it remind you of anything?"

"I've seen ground fog before, but this looks different somehow."

"Think back to your earlier remark about how much this place is how you imagined Eden to be."

Suddenly Randy snapped his finger. "That's it! Eden! It never rained in Eden either, did it? The garden was watered by moisture that rose from the ground."

"That's right. It says in Genesis, 'For the Lord God had not caused it to rain on the earth, and there was no man to till the ground; but a mist went up from the earth and watered the whole face of the ground.'"[87]

"Then this *is* Eden!" Randy exclaimed.

"I really don't know, Randy," Eli replied. "At the very least, it is a place where the Lord has recreated the conditions that existed in Eden, perhaps to give those who come here a taste of what it was like in the beginning and to stir in them a longing for its return."

"Well, it's working. The longer I stay here, the less I want to leave."

"No matter how often I come here, I always feel the same way."

———·—·———

After a simple supper of soup and sandwiches, Eli and Randy resumed their discussion. The sun was just dropping behind the western hills when they sat down with their Bibles on cushioned lawn chairs in a screened-in porch at the western side of the back of the cottage. Daylight was fading to dusk, but the rising moon was full and cast a bright glow into the porch where they were sitting. Birdsong had gone silent, replaced by the rhythmic chirping of crickets. It reminded Randy of the many warm, carefree summer nights he had enjoyed as a child.

Once again, Eli got things started.

"God created man and gave him the power of procreation because He wanted to fill the earth with a race of beings created in His own image. Creating man also served God's purpose to reveal His essential core nature of love. The greatest expression of His love was revealed in the death of His Son, Jesus Christ, for the sins of the world. It was important for God in creating mankind to make us free moral agents so that through trials and tests we could be purified and conformed to the image of Christ, and be made ready to rule and reign with Christ in eternity.

"How does all of this make you feel, Randy?"

Randy smiled. "For one thing, knowing the importance of human beings to God's plan and the love He has for us, I don't think I will ever feel small or insignificant again."

"I know just what you mean," Eli said, looking out at the darkening sky. "It's really sad how many people look at the world around them or the cosmos above them, and instead of observing the handiwork of God see only a vast and pointless universe and themselves an infinitesimally small speck by comparison—an 'accident' of nature, the product of millions of years of mindless evolution trapped in a life devoid of meaning. Is there any wonder the people of our world are so full of despair?"

"If only they knew of the personal God who loves them and wants them to know Him personally."

"Yes, for after all, that is another reason God created man: that we might have a personal relationship with Him as children to their Father."

"Speaking of God as a Father," Randy said, "that leads right into the fourth reason for God creating man. *God created man with the power of procreation so that He could father a genetic, biological Son and not a created son like Adam.* I have several questions about this one. For starters, why did God want a *biological* Son in the first place? What was His reason? And why didn't Adam qualify? Adam was created as a biological being, so what's the difference?"

"Those are all good questions. Let's see if we can 'unpack' this reason together so you can understand God's purpose better.

"First of all, let's talk about the fatherhood of God. God has always had the nature and character of a Father, but this aspect of His nature, like so many of God's attributes, has become known to man gradually, through God's progressive revelation of Himself. Only four times in the entire Old Testament is God referred to as a Father. Psalm 68:5 describes God as the 'father of the fatherless.' Malachi 2:10 asks, 'Have we not all one Father? Has not one God created us?' This, of course, is the 'universal fatherhood' of God in the sense that He is the 'Father' of all men because He created us. This, however, is different from the kind of fatherhood we're talking about.

"Psalm 89:26-27 gets closer to the idea: 'He shall cry to Me, "You are my Father, my God, and the rock of my salvation." Also I will make him My firstborn, the highest of the kings of the earth.' Although the context identifies these verses with David, this is also a prophetic messianic psalm that refers to Christ, who called God 'My Father,' and who was to God, 'My firstborn.' The fourth verse is Isaiah 9:6, which ascribes to Christ the titles 'Mighty God, Everlasting Father.' We'll talk about that verse more in a little while.

"The New Testament, however, is where the fatherhood of God is most fully revealed."

Randy said, "I guess the most obvious is the birth of Jesus Himself, who was called the 'Son of God.'"

"That's right. Nothing reveals God's fatherhood better than the birth of His Son. The New Testament refers to God as 'Father' over 200 times—more than 150 of them from the lips of Jesus Himself. Jesus repeatedly speaks of God as 'My Father,' or 'The Father.' In over 50 other places, the New Testament refers to God in the collective as 'Our Father.'

"In order to understand the fatherhood of God, we must understand what it means to say that Jesus is the 'Son of God.' Unless we get that understanding right, we will miss the boat on everything else. Randy, what does the phrase 'Son of God' mean to you as it applies to Jesus?"

"Jesus is the Son of God in that He is of the same 'essence' as God, His Father—co-existent, co-eternal, and divine. He is part of the eternal Godhead of Father, Son, and Holy Spirit, one God in three Persons. As the Son of God, He was born as a human; He took on a flesh-and-blood body so that He could demonstrate the

Father's love by dying for the sins of mankind. I think John 3:16 sums it up best: 'For God so loved the world that He gave His only begotten Son, that whoever believes in Him should not perish but have everlasting life.'"

"Very good. I'm glad you mentioned the humanity of Jesus, because that is crucial to understanding the fatherhood of God. It's not enough just to say that Jesus is the Son of God; we must understand that He is the *only begotten* Son of God. According to the Bible, all of us who are believers are sons of God, but only Jesus is the *begotten* Son of God. Jesus' 'begottenness' is what makes Him unique."

"Does the word *begotten* refer to Jesus' being God's Son in the biological sense?"

"Yes, in the same way that Matthew's Gospel begins with a list of 'begots,' outlining the human genealogy of Jesus: 'Abraham begot Isaac, Isaac begot Jacob,' and so forth. It is a word that speaks to the ordinary, natural process of human procreation.

"The New Testament writers, particularly John, are very explicit in stating that Jesus was the only begotten Son of God—the Son of God in a sense that no one else is God's son. John uses the phrase 'only begotten' in reference to Jesus five times: four times in his Gospel and once in his first Epistle. Three times—in Acts 13:33, Hebrews 1:5, and Hebrews 5:5—the writers apply the words of the second Psalm to Jesus: 'You are My Son, today I have begotten You.'[88]

"Probably the most explicit Old Testament reference to Jesus as the begotten Son of God is Isaiah 9:6-7, which I referred to earlier. Let's look at the whole passage now."

Finding the text, Randy read:

"For unto us a Child is born, unto us a Son is given; and the government will be upon His shoulder. And His name will be called Wonderful, Counselor, Mighty God, Everlasting Father, Prince of Peace. Of the increase of His government and peace there will be no end, upon the throne of David and over His kingdom, to order it and establish it with judgment and justice

from that time forward, even forever. The zeal of the Lord of hosts will perform this."[89]

"What words do you see in these verses that relate to human procreation?" Eli asked.

"Child, born, Son, and Father."

"That's right. The Hebrew word translated 'born' here is the same word that is translated elsewhere as 'begot' or 'begotten.' Isaiah was prophesying a physical, human birth that would bring into the world of mankind the Son of God, who would also be a human descendant of David and therefore an heir to the throne of David's kingdom. Remember that long ago God had promised David that one of his descendants would rule his kingdom forever.[90] That descendant was Jesus Christ."

"I know these verses refer to Jesus," Randy said, "but they also ascribe to Him the titles 'Mighty God' and 'Everlasting Father,' as you mentioned earlier. That's a little confusing to me. If He is the Son, how can He be the Father?"

"In the sense that they are both part of the Godhead—the eternal Trinity. It is as you said earlier, Randy; God the Father and God the Son are of the same essence. The Father and the Son are distinct Persons, but the Bible also teaches that Jesus and His Father are one. Jesus came in His Father's name to do His Father's will and, as Luke 2:49 says, to be about His father's business. When Philip, one of Jesus' disciples asked Jesus to show them the Father, Jesus answered, 'Have I been with you so long, and yet you have not known Me, Philip? He who has seen Me has seen the Father; so how can you say, "Show us the Father"'[91] In this sense, then, it is perfectly accurate for Isaiah 9:6 to refer to Jesus as 'Mighty God, Everlasting Father.'"

"Still, Eli, why did God need Jesus specifically as His Son? Why couldn't the angels fulfill God's fatherhood nature? Why couldn't Adam? After all, God created them all?"

Eli looked Randy in the eye. "I think you already know the answer to that question, Randy. The angels could not satisfy God's fatherly nature for the same reason they could not satisfy His love nature."

"Because they were not created in God's image and likeness!"

"Correct. Begetting involves procreation and procreation means producing others of the same kind. The angels, although created by God, are not like Him and so He cannot be their Father in this deeply personal sense."

"But Adam was like God—created in God's image and likeness. Why didn't Adam satisfy God's father nature?"

"Because Adam was created, not begotten."

Randy's face lit up with sudden comprehension. "Okay, now I understand the distinction."

"Right. God was Adam's father in a general sense through creation—just as He is the 'father' of all humans. But He was not Adam's father in the personal, biological sense of begetting him as a son. Adam was created from the dust of the earth, and Eve was formed from one of Adam's ribs. They alone out of the entire human race were not the product of normal human reproduction. Every other human who has ever lived, including Jesus, came to be through the normal process of procreation—conception, pre-natal growth and development, and birth."

"So God's fatherhood nature could be fully satisfied only by fathering a biological human child of His own. And before He could do that, He had to have a race of biological beings who were like Himself in image and likeness and endowed with the power of procreation."

"Exactly. We've already talked about Jesus being the 'second Adam,' completely sinless in contrast to the first Adam's corruption. Jesus is different from the first Adam in another significant way. Adam was created, but not begotten. Jesus, on the other hand, as one of the ancient creeds of the Church puts it, was 'begotten, not created.' Both of these characteristics are crucial to understanding both the nature of Jesus Christ and the fatherhood of God."

"How so?"

"As the second Person of the Godhead, Christ the Son is eternally co-existent with and the same essence of God the Father and therefore not created. In His human incarnation as Jesus of Nazareth, He was begotten of the Father through the normal process of human procreation. He is at once both fully divine and fully human—the 'God/man.' He now possesses a glorified, resurrected body that will be His throughout eternity, a body He did not have before He was born to Mary in Bethlehem. It was through Jesus' conception in Mary's womb by the Holy Spirit and birth by the normal procreative process of pregnancy and delivery that God fully satisfied His nature and desire to father a biological Son.'"

Randy tugged at his collar. "I have to confess, Eli, that some of this talk is starting to make me a little uncomfortable. You're not suggesting that God came down and had sexual intercourse with Mary, are you?"

"Absolutely not!" Eli declared. "This is an area where we must be very careful to be extremely precise in our explanation and understanding. Many pagan religions believed that the gods routinely had sex with humans. Even throughout the history of the Church, there have been various cults and sects that have believed that Mary conceived Jesus through having sex with God. Let me be absolutely clear here that the Bible does not teach that in any way, shape, or form. God is a Spirit being, and until Jesus was born, He had no physical body. And yet the Bible also clearly states that Mary conceived Jesus in her womb. You remember the story: the angel Gabriel came to Mary and said:

> 'Do not be afraid, Mary, for you have found favor with God. And behold, you will conceive in your womb and bring forth a Son, and shall call His name Jesus... The Holy Spirit will come upon you, and the power of the Highest will overshadow you; therefore, also, that Holy One who is to be born will be called the Son of God.'[92]

"Randy, how does human conception occur?"

"A sperm cell from the male fertilizes an egg from the female."

"Right; and it was no different with Jesus. Mary, who was a virgin, meaning she had never had sexual relations with a man, conceived Jesus when a sperm cell from God fertilized an egg from her ovary. Somehow, in a manner unknown to us, God implanted a sperm cell in her that contained His genetic makeup, His DNA.

"It is a known fact of human biology that a baby in the womb gets its blood from the father and not the mother. The mother's blood never mixes or comes into contact with the baby's blood. The blood that coursed through Jesus' veins was from His Father—God—not His mother, Mary. To say that Jesus was the only begotten Son of God is not figurative language, but *literal*. In some way that we cannot fathom, God became the *literal* and *biological* Father of Jesus. I simply see no other way to interpret the biblical language."

Randy said, "I still find it amazing that God would create an entire race—an entire planet full of people—just so He could biologically father one Son of His own."

"Don't forget, Randy, that this reason for creating mankind is linked to the others we have already discussed: God's desire to fill the earth with beings in His own image and likeness, His desire to express His love nature by suffering, bleeding, and dying for our sins—for which He needed a mortal human body—and His desire for a race of free moral agents who are tested, purified, and prepared to reign with Him in eternity. God's overall plan calls for an entire race of beings, not just a few or one or two."

"I guess that lends even more importance then, to man being given the power of procreation."

"Indeed it does. As a matter of fact, mankind's ability to procreate is central to all God's reasons for creating us that we have discussed so far. God wanted us to have procreative power so that He would have a means for fathering a biological Son through conception and birth. He wanted us to procreate so that He could obtain a human body through which he could suffer, bleed, and die for us and reveal His nature of love. With that body, Jesus, the Son of God, modeled God's ideal type of true mankind being. At the same time, that body would become the perfect sacrifice for sin. Jesus was God's perfect man and man's perfect God. None of that would have been possible without a body, and a body would not have been possible without mankind's ability to procreate.

"Look back at Luke 1:35, where Gabriel said to Mary, 'The Holy Spirit will come upon you, and the power of the Highest will overshadow you; therefore, also, that Holy One who is to be born will be called the Son of God.' What 'power of the Highest' was going to overshadow her?"

"The power to become pregnant without knowing a man?"

"Yes, or in other words, the power of procreation—in this case, God's procreative power. That power provided the sperm cell, enabled Mary to conceive and, nine months later, to give birth to God's human, biological Son, Jesus. The coming of Jesus was not so much a miraculous birth as it was a miraculous conception. Jesus' birth was by perfectly normal and natural processes; His conception was not. God did not 'speak' Jesus into Mary's womb; He enabled her to conceive through the fertilization of an egg by a sperm cell. The conception of Jesus was a miracle—a *biological* miracle.

"We cannot overestimate the importance of the 'begottenness' of Jesus. Very simply, if Jesus was not begotten of God, then God is not His Father. The truth is, however, that Jesus is the only begotten Son of God. His is the only human body that God ever fathered. He is the only mortal, physical, biological being that God ever fathered, or ever will. Jesus is the *only* begotten Son of God."

"But why did God wait so long? I mean, if He wanted to satisfy His fatherly nature, why did He wait thousands of years before bringing His Son into the world?"

"The nature of God's plan is such that it must be worked out over time which, as you will remember, is significant only to us. Time means nothing to God in eternity, except as it serves to bring His plan to pass. Let's look at Galatians 4:4-5."

Randy read: "But when the fullness of the time had come, God sent forth His Son, born of a woman, born under the law, to redeem those who were under the law, that we might receive the adoption as sons."

"'The fullness of time' is a significant phrase in the Bible. Everything God does has a purpose, and it is always timely—never early and never late. God's plan always comes to pass 'in the fullness

CREATED SO THAT GOD COULD FATHER HIS OWN BIOLOGICAL SON

of time'; in other words, when God has determined that the time is right. He determined before the world began that His Son would die on a cross for the sins of mankind, but that event had to wait until the time was right—the 'fullness of time' in God's plan. According to this verse, what happened in the 'fullness of time'?"

"God's Son came forth, 'born of a woman, born under the law.'"

"In other words, born as a human under the same law that governed mankind. What was His purpose in coming?"

"To redeem those who were under the law that they—that *we*—might receive adoption as sons."

"Do you see the connection here, Randy? This was God's plan all along, to father a biological Son 'in the fullness of time' so that He could redeem lost humanity to Himself, adopting us as sons and therefore gathering for Himself a great family—a *human* family."

Randy nodded.

"So, through the creation of man, God fulfilled three desires: His desire for a family, His desire for His Son to take on a human body and be our God forever, and His desire to fashion human, bodily temples as a dwelling place for His Spirit."

"If I understand you correctly," Randy said, "the begetting of Jesus and the gathering of a human family are inseparably linked in the mind and plan of God and have been since the very beginning."

"Absolutely. Let's look at some Scriptures to back it up. First, John 1:1-5."

Randy read:

"In the beginning was the Word, and the Word was with God, and the Word was God. He was in the beginning with God. All things were made through Him, and without Him nothing was made that was made. In Him was life, and the life was the light of men. And the light shines in the darkness, and the darkness did not comprehend it."[93]

"Randy, God and His Word are one. And His greatest Word, the supreme example of His self-expression, was Jesus Christ His Son, who has been with Him from the beginning and is of the same essence as He. Christ is the source of life and spiritual light for mankind. Now read verses 12-14."

"But as many as received Him, to them He gave the right to become children of God, to those who believe in His name: who were born, not of blood, nor of the will of the flesh, nor of the will of man, but of God. And the Word became flesh and dwelt among us, and we beheld His glory, the glory as of the only begotten of the Father, full of grace and truth."[94]

"To all who receive Jesus—who 'believe in His name' and trust Him as their Lord and Savior—He gives the right to become children of God. *Children* of God implies a *family* of God. Just as we are born into our human family, we must also be born into God's family. The difference, of course, is that the first is a physical birth while the second is a spiritual birth. This is what Jesus meant when He told Nicodemus, 'Unless one is born again, he cannot see the kingdom of God...Unless one is born of water and the Spirit, he cannot enter the kingdom of God. That which is born of the flesh is flesh, and that which is born of the Spirit is spirit. Do not marvel that I said to you, "You must be born again."'[95]

"God's method for building His family was to send His Son, who 'became flesh and dwelt among us' with a glory 'as of the only begotten of the Father, full of grace and truth.' If the Son of God had never come in the flesh, we would never be able to become children of God, and God would never have the family He desires. All these things are related in His plan. It all hinges on the truth that Jesus is the 'only begotten'—the unique biological—Son of God. Read verse 18."

"No one has seen God at any time. The only begotten Son, who is in the bosom of the Father, He has declared Him."[96]

"Jesus had no earthly biological father. Joseph was Jesus' stepfather. God Himself was Jesus' biological Father, and it is through Jesus that we come to know the Father. Jesus is the only begotten Son of God. The physical, resurrected, glorified body of Jesus is the only physical expression or form of God that we will ever see. In

Christ, God has chosen us, as well as all others who believe, to be part of His great family, a human, genetic family rather than just a created family."

"So what you're saying, then," Randy interjected, "is that Jesus, the only begotten Son of God, was born on earth as a human being in order to show us what God the Father is like so that we could know Him and become His children."

"Exactly. The New Testament generally uses the phrase 'sons of God,' to refer to all believers, and the phrase 'bride of Christ' as a synonym for 'Church.' Some people have a problem with the apparent gender-specific nature of these terms, but they shouldn't. 'Sons of God' and 'bride of Christ' are not talking about male and female but about our relationship to God. 'Sons' refers to our kinship to God as His rightful and legal children and heirs, just as sons in the ancient world were heirs to their father's estate. 'Bride' refers to the intimacy of the marriage relationship, which is a picture of the kind of spiritual intimacy we can have with Christ. The emphasis here is not on gender but *relationship*.

"Just as Jesus had a natural birth that made Him the Son of God in the flesh, so we have a spiritual birth that makes us a son of God in the spirit. Tell me, Randy, can you become a child of God simply by agreeing with Christian tenets of faith and doctrine? Can you become a child of God simply by accepting certain beliefs and creeds, changing your lifestyle and going to church, and being baptized into that system?"

"No," Randy replied. "Of course not. You have to be born again, just as Jesus said."

"Does 'born again' refer to a natural or a spiritual birth?"

"A spiritual birth."

"That's right. There are no 'naturalized' citizens in God's kingdom; only native-born citizens. In a very real sense there is no such thing as 'joining' the Church. The Church is the body of Christ and we must be born into it through the new birth that Jesus talks about in the third chapter of John. Nicodemus, the Pharisee and legal expert, had trouble understanding what Jesus was saying because he was thinking in terms of natural birth only. The concept of spiritual birth was completely new to him. That is why Jesus clarified the matter by saying, 'Unless one is born of water and the Spirit, he cannot enter the kingdom of God. That which is born of the flesh is flesh, and that which is born of the Spirit is spirit.'"

"Eli, you mentioned that there are no 'naturalized' citizens in God's kingdom, but only those who are 'native-born.' I've also heard it said that 'God has no stepchildren.'"

"That is entirely correct. Every child of God is His by *birth*; a direct 'bloodline' relation, you might say. What does Second Corinthians 5:17 say?"

Randy nodded even as he looked up the verse. "I know that one," he said. Finding the place, he read, "'Therefore, if anyone is in Christ, he is a new creation; old things have passed away; behold, all things have become new.'"

"What does it mean to be a 'new creation'?"

"When we trust Christ as our Savior and Lord and have our sins cleansed by His blood, we are 'born again' spiritually. We become a 'new creation' in Christ, just as a newborn baby is a new human creation that has come into the world."

"Very good. Being born again also means being born *directly* into God's family. It means having a new nature—a 'new you'—birthed into your life, a new nature that loves God and lives to please and honor Him. The goal of our new nature is to become like Jesus. He is the perfect model and example of what our 'new man' should be like. God's purpose and desire is for all of His children to grow up to be like Jesus in character, faith, and obedience.

"In order to fulfill God's purpose for our lives, we must be born again. We must become a 'new creation' in Christ. Apart from that, nothing else matters. Unless we become new creations and are born into God's eternal family, we will miss out on His will and purpose for us. Paul stated plainly the critical importance of the new birth: 'For in Christ Jesus neither circumcision nor uncircumcision avails anything, but a new creation.'[97] Becoming a new creation is the only thing that avails with God. Changing our lifestyle, trying to be good and do the right thing, going to church, tithing; all of these things are important in their place, but they mean nothing for eternity without the first step of becoming a new creation in Christ."

"If Jesus is God's biological, begotten Son, and therefore unique, how can we become like Him? We don't have God's 'DNA.'"

"You're quite right, Randy," Eli replied. We do not have God's 'DNA' in the sense that Jesus does. Nevertheless, as new creations in Christ, we are children of God and can take on His characteristics. Think about it this way: we all inherit genetic traits from our parents. We share DNA, certain physical characteristics such as hair color, eye color, height, build, and sometimes even the propensity for certain hereditary health conditions. These common characteristics become more prominent as we grow. Over time, we generally become like our parents in many ways, not just physically but also in our beliefs, values, attitudes, and behavior.

"It is the same way when we are born again as children of God. The Holy Spirit comes to live in us and imparts to us the spiritual characteristics—God's 'DNA' as it were—that will cause us to become more and more like Jesus as we grow in our faith. I'm talking about such things as spiritual gifts and the fruit of the Spirit, as well as His righteousness, holiness, and character—in short, His nature. When we are born into God's family, He gives us everything we need to grow up to be like Him."

"Why is it then that so many Christians are so little like Jesus?"

"That's a good question. There are many reasons. One is simple ignorance. Many Christians either do not know or do not understand the legacy they have in Christ. Since they have never been taught that they can be like Christ, they never try. Instead, their lives are unsatisfying and lacking peace and spiritual power, and they never really know why.

"For many other Christians, the biggest problem is that their main goal is to get to Heaven, while God's main goal is to conform them to the image of Christ. Their vision and direction are wrong. They concentrate on trying to get through life with as few difficulties and trials as possible. If our focus is on getting to Heaven, we are focused on the wrong thing. God will take care of the business of getting us to Heaven if we will get serious about the business of being conformed to Christ's image.

"Still other Christians are lazy. Becoming like Christ requires too much effort, too much work, and too much discipline. They would rather take it easy. Then there are those whose hearts are still in rebellion. Every day is a struggle for them in denying the old man and saying yes to the new man in them. Many more Christians, however, are simply still in training. To an outside observer, they may not look or act much like Jesus today, but they do more so than yesterday. All of us are in process of becoming. It is easier for some than for others because some are more willing to pay the price."

"Is this why our free will is so important?"

"Yes. God gave us free will because freedom of choice is part of being created in His image. We discussed that when we talked about humans being free moral agents. God wants us to be like Jesus, but He will not force us. God sent His Son to earth because He wanted to bring forth from every tribe, kindred, and nation many human beings who are redeemed by the blood of Jesus. His goal is to build a family of multi-millions of redeemed men and women. Many in this family will pay the price and grow to maturity as sons and daughters of God who are ready and able to rule and reign with Christ over His vast domain throughout the endless ages of eternity.

"Jesus was the only begotten Son of God by birth, but we can become 'begotten' sons of God through a spiritual birth. That opportunity is available to anyone who will believe and accept it. All who receive Jesus Christ as their personal Savior and Lord also receive from Him the power and privilege to become the sons of God. This was God's plan from the beginning. Read Romans 8:28-30."

Randy read:

"And we know that all things work together for good to those who love God, to those who are the called according to His purpose. For whom He foreknew, He also predestined to be conformed to the image of His Son, that He might be the firstborn among many brethren. Moreover whom He predestined, these

He also called; whom He called, these He also justified; and whom He justified, these He also glorified."[98]

"Verse 29 says that Jesus is the 'firstborn among many brethren.' Who are His brethren?"

"Everyone who believes; all Christians."

"Right. And God, in His foreknowledge and omniscience, knew from the very beginning who would believe and who would not. From the very beginning God predestined that all who believe would be conformed to the image of His Son.

"God wanted a family drawn from every race, kindred, and nation. As the family of God, all believers are 'blood kin' of Jesus and, therefore, of each other. All born-again believers are members of the same 'race,' the 'Church race,' the bride and body of Christ. There are no more divisions into the Anglo race or the African race or the Asian race. Gone is the distinction of color and nationality because we are all one in Jesus. Paul wrote:

'For you are all sons of God through faith in Christ Jesus. For as many of you as were baptized into Christ have put on Christ. There is neither Jew nor Greek, there is neither slave nor free, there is neither male nor female; for you are all one in Christ Jesus. And if you are Christ's, then you are Abraham's seed, and heirs according to the promise."[99]

"It is because we are all one in Christ Jesus that racism is such a sin and so completely out of place among Christians. By making us one, Christ tore down all the barriers that otherwise divide us. The Church is the family of God. Just as we as individual believers should pattern our lives after Christ and model God's kind of man (or woman), the Church should portray to the world God's kind of family."

"Eli, you just said that we should pattern our lives after Christ. I know that means to live with the goal of becoming like Him, and that Bible study and prayer and worship are all keys to that, but what else is involved? How else do we become like Jesus?"

"One way is by being faithful to be in regular fellowship with one another. We grow and learn from each other. Another way is by learning to identify as completely as possible with Jesus and what He experienced while on earth. If we claim to be joint heirs with Jesus we have to be ready to identify with Him in every way. Paul stated it this way:

> 'For you did not receive the spirit of bondage again to fear, but you received the Spirit of adoption by whom we cry out, "Abba, Father." The Spirit Himself bears witness with our spirit that we are children of God, and if children, then heirs—heirs of God and joint heirs with Christ, if indeed we suffer with Him, that we may also be glorified together.'[100]

"Notice the key phrase, 'if indeed we suffer with Him.' Does that remind you of anything we have talked about so far?"

"Yes, about our being free moral agents and the tests and trials we go through to purify us, bring us to maturity, and prepare us to reign with Christ."

"That's right. If we are joint heirs with Christ and hope to reign with Him in eternity, we must be prepared to go through what He went through—both good and bad. We cannot truly identify with His reign if we refuse to identify with His suffering."

"That's not a pleasant subject."

"No it isn't, and many Christians would rather ignore it. Nevertheless, suffering for Christ is inescapable for all who are serious about following Him and reigning with Him. Paul told Timothy, 'All who desire to live godly in Christ Jesus will suffer persecution.'[101] Learning to persevere under persecution and remain faithful through trials will shape us into the likeness of Christ more than anything else will."

"Why do so many Christians seem not to understand this?"

"Either they are under leadership that does not teach it, or they choose not to believe it. They want the blessings but not the burdens and the power but not the pressure. They would rather stay in the mountaintop retreat with Jesus than go with Him into the get-your-hands-dirty work in the valley. Believers who hold such an attitude will never reach full maturity."

"God desires all of us to become mature," Randy said, "but because we are all free moral agents, He won't force the issue."

"That's right. The choice is ours. If we choose not to identify with Jesus all the way, come what may, we'll still get to Heaven but we will miss out on much that God planned and desired for us. His plan from the beginning has been to build a family in the image of His Son who would be fit to rule with Him. God created the human race so that He could father a biological Son, Jesus Christ, who would then suffer, bleed, and die for the sins of mankind. In so doing, Christ would 'bring many sons to glory'[102] by making them children of God where they could be molded into His likeness.

"This family of God is the Church, known also as both the body and the bride of Christ. There is much we have to discuss about the Church, because it too is one of the reasons for the creation of the human race. But that is a discussion that can wait until tomorrow."

6

CREATED TO BE
THE BRIDE OF CHRIST

Randy awoke to another beautiful sunrise, the sun shining bright and clear in a gloriously blue and cloudless sky as it ascended from behind the distant hills to the east. As Randy lay quietly in the peace and serenity of the moment, his mind jumped inexplicably to thoughts of home. "This is my third day here," he thought. "I'm missing a lot of classes. I wonder if anyone has reported me missing. I hope Mom and Dad aren't worried about me."

Yet, even as he lay there, Randy found himself unable to worry about the situation. There was something about this place; fear or worry simply could not get a foothold. It was as though they were barred from entry. It was a sensation Randy had never known before. Somehow, he knew, when all this was over, everything would be okay. Besides, he was convinced that the time he was spending with Eli was more important than anything he could be doing at home. In spite of himself, Randy was completely at peace.

———··———

After breakfast, Randy and Eli again met in the parlor for their morning discussion.

"I think this morning we will be focusing on a lot of Scripture," Eli began, "but first, let's see where we have come so far. Randy, describe for me in your own words why God created the human race."

Randy gathered his thoughts for a few moments, took a deep breath, and plunged in.

"God created man in His own image and likeness. He made them male and female and gave them the power of procreation because He wanted to fill the earth with an entire race of beings who were like Himself in character and behavior. By God's design, all humans are free moral agents who are free to choose whether to obey God or to reject Him. Our free moral agency is necessary in order for us to be tried, tested, purified, and matured in preparation for ruling and reigning with Christ in eternity.

"God's creation of man also gave Him the opportunity to fully express His love nature by making it possible for Him to take on human flesh and suffer, bleed, and die for our sins. This He accomplished by fathering His own biological Son, Jesus Christ, who was conceived by the Holy Spirit and born of the virgin Mary. This fulfilled God's fatherly nature, not only His desire for an only begotten Son of His own, but also His desire for an eternal family, because all who believe in and receive Christ as Savior and Lord are born into His family and become children of God. As such, all believers are heirs of God and joint heirs with Jesus, comprising one great family of God that will endure forever."

Eli smiled and nodded with satisfaction. "Excellent summary, Randy! You are grasping these concepts extremely well. The next reason we are going to discuss, I believe, builds on what you just said about all believers being a family of God. That family is also called the Church and the body of Christ. There is another name that the New Testament gives to the family of God, a name that is the central element of God's fifth reason for creating the human race. What is that reason?"

"God created man in order to provide a many-membered bride for His Son."

"That sounds simple, doesn't it? But there is a lot of meaning wrapped up in that word *bride*. What can you tell me about the meaning of the phrase, 'bride of Christ'?"

"Well, for one thing, I know that it is a reference to the Church. The New Testament calls the Church the bride of Christ. I have to admit, however, that I have never really understood what that means. Maybe it's because I'm not married. But I have also heard different Bible teachers say different things. Some say that the Church is the bride of Christ while others say that the phrase refers to Israel. Still others offer different interpretations. There doesn't seem to be clear or universal agreement as to who constitutes the bride of Christ."

"You are correct on all counts. Some controversy does exist among theologians and preachers as to the identity of the bride of Christ. Most hold the belief that it is the Church, but some believe that Israel is the bride while the Church is the *friend* of the bride. There are others who hold that Israel is the wife of God because He was married to Israel by covenant, and that the Church is the bride of Christ. The problem with that view is that it implies two distinctly different beings in the Godhead, and we have already seen that there is only one God—one spiritual being in essence and nature who nevertheless manifests Himself in three distinct Persons: Father, Son, and Holy Spirit.

"I want us to focus on a number of Scriptures that will give ample proof that the Church is the bride of Christ. But first, let me ask you a question: Why didn't Jesus get married while He was here in His mortal body? Marriage was the accepted and expected norm for young men of His age. Rabbis and teachers, as Jesus was, especially were expected to marry. Why didn't Jesus?"

"Jesus' purpose in coming to earth was not to marry and raise a family, but to die on the cross as the Lamb of God, the ultimate and final sacrifice to take away the sins of the world."

"That is true, but there is another reason as well, one that is related to what we are already talking about."

Randy's eyes lit up. "The Church! We're the bride of Christ. Jesus never married while on earth because He already had a bride!"

"Exactly. God the Father had already planned a bride for His Son, a many-membered body of redeemed mankind. Jesus could not marry during His time on earth because He was already 'taken.' He was already betrothed to His bride, the Church. In a little while we will see why Jesus needs a many-membered bride—a bride made up of millions of redeemed human beings—rather than one single person. For the moment, let's see what the Bible says about the Church as the bride of Christ. Look at Isaiah 56:5."

Finding the passage, Randy read: "'Even to them I will give in My house and within My walls a place and a name better than that of sons and daughters; I will give them an everlasting name that shall not be cut off.'[103] What does that have to do with the bride of Christ?"

"Let's interpret this verse in light of the New Testament. In this verse God is speaking about His people and He says He will give them 'a place and a name better than that of sons and daughters.' As believers, we are the children of God. What 'place' has He given us?"

"A place in Heaven?"

"Good; you're close. Ephesians 2:6 says that God has raised us up to sit 'in the heavenly places in Christ Jesus.' What name has He given us? How are we who are followers of Christ known?"

"Christians?"

"Right. The Book of Acts says that the followers of Jesus were first called Christians in Antioch.[104] A Christian is someone who belongs to Christ. What is better than being called a son or a daughter? In other words, what relationship is closer and more intimate?"

"Husband and wife?"

"Yes; or bride and groom. There is a oneness that exists between husband and wife that does not exist between parents and children. That is why the Bible says that when a man and a woman come together as husband and wife they become 'one flesh.' Also, there is the question of inheritance. Sons and daughters receive a portion of the inheritance, but the bride receives everything. In John 14:2-3 Jesus says that His Father's house has many 'mansions' and that He goes to prepare a place for us. Our 'mansion' is not a house in Heaven but our membership ministry in the body of Christ. Let's look now at Psalm 45:9."

Again, Randy read: "'Kings' daughters are among Your honorable women; at Your right hand stands the queen in gold from Ophir.'[105] Okay, Eli, what does *this* one mean?"

"Psalm 45 is another messianic psalm that talks about the King and His Queen. Again, interpreting from the framework of the New Testament, we know that the Church is the bride of Christ. If Christ is the King, then the Church—His bride—must be the queen."

Randy nodded. "That makes sense."

"Turn now to the Song of Solomon. This book is widely regarded as extolling the joys of human marital love, but many also see it as an allegorical or symbolic picture of Christ's relationship to His Church—His bride. Find chapter four and read verses 8-12, and then the first verse of chapter five."

"Come with me from Lebanon, my spouse, with me from Lebanon. Look from the top of Amana, from the top of Senir and Hermon, from the lions' dens, from the mountains of the leopards. You have ravished my heart, my sister, my spouse; you have ravished my heart with one look of your eyes, with one link of your necklace. How fair is your love, my sister, my spouse! How much better than wine is your love, and the scent of your perfumes than all spices! Your lips, O my spouse, drip as the honeycomb; honey and milk are under your tongue; and the fragrance of your garments is like the fragrance of Lebanon. A garden enclosed is my sister, my spouse, a spring shut up, a fountain sealed... I have come to my garden, my sister, my spouse; I have gathered my myrrh with my spice; I have eaten my honeycomb with my honey; I have drunk my wine with my milk."[106]

Eli caught Randy's questioning look. "I know the word 'bride' does not appear anywhere in these verses. Substitute 'bride' everywhere you see the word 'spouse.' First of all, in the context of the passage, it is the King, or the Bridegroom, who is speaking of His 'spouse'; in other words, His bride. Second of all, the Hebrew word *kallah*, which is translated 'spouse,' also means 'bride,' and is translated that way in many other Bible versions. If Song of Solomon symbolizes Christ and His Church, there can be no doubt, from this book alone, that the Church is the bride of Christ.

"Also," Eli continued, "verse 12 speaks of the bride as an enclosed garden, a shut-up spring and a sealed fountain. These descriptions relate in an important way to the idea of the Church as the bride of Christ, but we will return to them later. For now, let's continue examining Scriptures. Turn back to Isaiah again. Read Isaiah 49:16."

"See, I have inscribed you on the palms of My hands; your walls are continually before Me."[107]

"This chapter of Isaiah speaks of the Messiah, and in this particular verse, the Messiah is talking about Zion, or Jerusalem, which stands for the people of God. Again, by New Testament extension, this means the Church. We are as close to Him as if physically engraved on His hand, just as close as a bride is to her husband. Look now at Isaiah 61:10."

"I will greatly rejoice in the Lord, my soul shall be joyful in my God; for He has clothed me with the garments of salvation, He has covered me with the robe of righteousness, as a bridegroom decks himself with ornaments, and as a bride adorns herself with her jewels."[108]

"Isaiah 62:5."

"For as a young man marries a virgin, so shall your sons marry you; and as the bridegroom rejoices over the bride, so shall your God rejoice over you."[109]

"Randy, can you see how prominent this imagery of the bride and groom is in depicting the Lord's relationship with His people?"

"Yes. I never realized how often it appears in the Old Testament. I'm more familiar with the references in Revelation."

"Most people are. Before we go there, however, let's look at some other New Testament references to the bride of Christ. First, John 3:28-30."

"You yourselves bear me witness, that I said, 'I am not the Christ,' but, 'I have been sent before Him.' He who has the bride is the bridegroom; but the friend of the bridegroom, who stands and hears him, rejoices greatly because of the bridegroom's voice.

Therefore this joy of mine is fulfilled. He must increase, but I must decrease."[110]

"John the Baptist is speaking here and the 'bridegroom' he refers to is Jesus, who 'has the bride.' John refers to himself as the 'friend of the bridegroom,' and although John is rightly regarded as the last of the Old Testament prophets, he was also part of the bride because he believed in Jesus.

"Moving beyond the Gospels, let's see what Paul had to say about the bride of Christ. Turn to Romans 7:4."

"Therefore, my brethren, you also have become dead to the law through the body of Christ, that you may be married to another—to Him who was raised from the dead, that we should bear fruit to God."[111]

"Paul's language couldn't be any plainer: as believers, we are to be married to Christ. We are His bride. Go to Second Corinthians 11:2."

"For I am jealous for you with godly jealousy. For I have betrothed you to one husband, that I may present you as a chaste virgin to Christ."[112]

"Who is the 'chaste virgin' whom Paul has 'betrothed' to Christ?"

"The believers in Corinth—the Corinthian Church."

"Yes. Through Paul's preaching they had become believers in Christ, joining all other believers everywhere in becoming betrothed to Him as His many-membered bride. Now, three references in the Book of Revelation, and that ought to be sufficient. First, Revelation 19:7."

"Let us be glad and rejoice and give Him glory, for the marriage of the Lamb has come, and His wife has made herself ready."[113]

"Good; now, Revelation 21:1-2."

"Now I saw a new heaven and a new earth, for the first heaven and the first earth had passed away. Also there was no more sea. Then I, John, saw the holy city, New Jerusalem, coming down

out of heaven from God, prepared as a bride adorned for her husband."[114]

"And finally, Revelation 21:9-11a."

"Then one of the seven angels who had the seven bowls filled with the seven last plagues came to me and talked with me, saying, 'Come, I will show you the bride, the Lamb's wife.' And he carried me away in the Spirit to a great and high mountain, and showed me the great city, the holy Jerusalem, descending out of heaven from God, having the glory of God."[115]

"In all three of these passages, the context makes it clear that the bride of Christ is the Church. The city called 'New Jerusalem' descending from Heaven is a symbolic reference to the Church. Just as the earthly city of Jerusalem represents Israel, God's chosen people under the Mosaic covenant, so the heavenly Jerusalem represents the Church, the family of God under the new covenant in Christ's blood."

"I see what you mean," Randy said. "It is pretty clear that the Church is the bride of Christ. None of these verses we have looked at imply in any way that the bride of Christ is anything less than or other than the full and complete body of the children of God."

"And that will become even more apparent the further we go."

"Eli, I've heard some teachers say that the Church as the body and bride of Christ was an afterthought with God. According to them, God's original plan involved the nation of Israel, but when they blew it through disobedience and rebellion, God had to come up with 'Plan B': the Church. That always sounded a little fishy to me because I don't believe God is ever taken by surprise. The Scriptures we have examined so far seem to confirm that God had the Church in mind as the bride of Christ from the very start."

"You're correct, Randy. Nothing ever surprises God. He doesn't need a 'Plan B' because His original plan is still in operation and it will be fulfilled. As you said, the Church was in His mind and plan from the beginning. The Bible is very clear about this. In fact, we can see in the relationship between Adam and Eve a type or prototype of Christ's relationship with His Church. Read Genesis 2:23-24."

"And Adam said: 'This is now bone of my bones and flesh of my flesh; she shall be called Woman, because she was taken out of Man.' Therefore a man shall leave his father and mother and be joined to his wife, and they shall become one flesh."[116]

"Woman was 'taken out of Man,' and when they come together as husband and wife, they become 'one flesh.' Both of those phrases are images of intimacy, and describe perfectly the intimate nature of our relationship with Christ as His bride. Just as woman was taken out of Man's side, so also the Church, the bride of Christ was taken out of the Man Christ Jesus through His blood. With His own blood Jesus purchased the redemption of His bride.

"As the bride of Christ, we were chosen by God long before we were ever born. Read Ephesians 1:3-4."

"Blessed be the God and Father of our Lord Jesus Christ, who has blessed us with every spiritual blessing in the heavenly places in Christ, just as He chose us in Him before the foundation of the world, that we should be holy and without blame before Him in love."[117]

"God chose us in Christ *before* the foundation of the world. The Church—Christ's bride– was not an afterthought in God's mind. Just as with all the other reasons we have discussed, God had a bride for His Son in His plans before He ever created the human race. God is neither impulsive nor random; everything He does has a purpose. Before man was even around to choose to sin, God knew He wanted to create a race of beings in His image and likeness who would possess free moral agency and the power of procreation. He knew He wanted to father a biological Son through that race who would have a human body like theirs so He could suffer, bleed, and die for their sins. He knew He wanted a bride for His Son, and that He would redeem millions of beings from that race and present them as a many-membered bride for His Son. No afterthought; just one amazing and incredible plan. Now read Titus 1:2."

"In hope of eternal life which God, who cannot lie, promised before time began."[118]

"Who has the hope of eternal life?"

"All who believe in Christ."

"Yes, and collectively, those believers are called the Church and the bride of Christ. So again we see how God had all of this planned from the start, because He promised the hope of eternal life 'before time began.' Only those who are 'in Christ,' as Paul says in Ephesians, will have eternal life. Some people claim that all religions are valid; that all roads lead to the same place. In a way, they do; all roads lead to the judgment seat of Christ. Only the road from the cross leads into Heaven, however; all other roads end up in hell.

"As a matter of fact, bringing forth a bride for His Son was at the very center of God's design and intention in creation. Everything that exists was created to bring about this end: to provide a bride for the Son of God."

Randy shook his head in amazement. "That sounds almost too incredible to believe."

"Doesn't it?" Eli stood up, walked over to the bookshelf and withdrew a small volume. "Let me read a quote to you written by a man who expresses it better than I can. He is a prophet who has spent many years pondering these things." Opening to the proper page, Eli read:

"The human *race* was created in the image and likeness of God *for one purpose: to provide an eternal companion for the Son.* After the fall and promise of redemption through the coming Messiah, *the Messianic race (Israel)* was born and nurtured in order to bring the *Messiah. And the Messiah came for one intent and only one: to give birth to His Church,* thus to obtain His Bride. *The Church* then—the called-out body of redeemed mankind—turns out to be *the central object, the goal,* not only of mundane history but of all that God has been doing in all realms, from all *eternity.*"[119]

There was a distant look in Randy's eyes. "It's hard to imagine that all of creation exists just so we could be here and be part of the family of God; members of the bride of Christ."

"I agree, it is hard to fathom," Eli said. "God created the universe and sent His Son to earth to die so that He could have *you* in

His family. Now *that's* something to think about the next time you feel small or insignificant!"

Randy nodded silently, still trying to take it in. After a few moments he said, "Earlier you mentioned that Adam and Eve's relationship was a prototype of Christ and His Church. Doesn't Paul make a similar comparison with regard to marriage?"

"Indeed he does, Randy, especially in the fifth chapter of Ephesians. Let's take a look. Why don't you read Ephesians 5:22-32."

Quickly opening to the passage, Randy read:

"Wives, submit to your own husbands, as to the Lord. For the husband is head of the wife, as also Christ is head of the church; and He is the Savior of the body. Therefore, just as the church is subject to Christ, so let the wives be to their own husbands in everything. Husbands, love your wives, just as Christ also loved the church and gave Himself for her, that He might sanctify and cleanse her with the washing of water by the word, that He might present her to Himself a glorious church, not having spot or wrinkle or any such thing, but that she should be holy and without blemish. So husbands ought to love their own wives as their own bodies; he who loves his wife loves himself. For no one ever hated his own flesh, but nourishes and cherishes it, just as the Lord does the church. For we are members of His body, of His flesh and of His bones. 'For this reason a man shall leave his father and mother and be joined to his wife, and the two shall become one flesh.' This is a great mystery, but I speak concerning Christ and the church."[120]

"In this passage, Paul gives explicit instructions regarding the attitude husbands and wives are to hold toward each other, yet also states in verse 32 that he is speaking of Christ and the Church. In other words, the relationship that exists between Christian husbands and wives should be a reflection of the relationship that exists between Jesus Christ and His bride, the Church. Paul says that husbands should love their wives as Christ loved the Church. How did Christ show His love for the Church, His bride?"

"He gave Himself for the Church. Jesus died for His bride."

"Yes, and for what purpose?"

"To redeem her for Himself."

"That's right. Look at the words Paul uses to describe the bride of Christ: 'sanctify,' 'cleanse,' 'glorious,' no 'spot or wrinkle,' 'holy,' 'without blemish.' Even though Paul uses the word 'church' in these verses, they still make sense if we substitute the word 'bride.' Christ gave Himself for the Church to sanctify and cleanse her and present her to Himself as a glorious *bride*, fit to reign in Heaven with the King as His Queen.

"Paul also plainly states that we are 'members of [Christ's] body, of His flesh and of His bones,' pointing out how intimately connected we are with Christ. He even quotes Genesis 2:24 about a husband and wife being 'one flesh.' Can there be any doubt that Christ loves His bride?

"Look back at verse 23. What does it say about Christ?"

"Christ is the head of the Church and the Savior of the body."

"Who is the Church?"

"We are."

"And who is the body?"

"We are."

"So then Christ is both our head and our Savior. We are both His bride and His body. Paul says that as members of Christ's body we are 'of His flesh and of His bones.' What does that mean?"

Randy pondered Eli's question for a few moments. "It means that we, the Church, the bride of Christ, are His flesh and bone body on the earth, kept by Him and called to do His work until He returns to take us to Himself."

"Very good. I asked that question because it is important to understand the difference between the body of Jesus and the body of Christ. The Bible never refers to the Church as the body of Jesus, but only as the body of Christ. Do you know why?"

"The body of Jesus refers to the specific physical body of the man named Jesus who was the human incarnation of the Son of God."

"And where is the body of Jesus now?"

"In Heaven with God the Father."

"Yes. And we are the spiritual body of Christ here on earth; spiritual beings in God's image and likeness inhabiting physical flesh and bone bodies so that we can carry on the work that Christ began when He walked the earth as Jesus of Nazareth. I also like how you referred to the return of Christ. Some day Jesus Christ will return to the earth physically and visibly in His resurrected and glorified body and gather us to His side as His bride to consummate the marriage. This is important to know because a couple of generations ago an erroneous teaching went out from some in the Church to the effect that there would be no visible, bodily return of Jesus. This teaching, called the 'extreme manifest sons of God,' held that when Jesus comes again He will return not visibly and physically, but simply be glorified in His saints. In other words, all anyone would ever 'see' of Christ is that which was revealed or 'manifested' in the lives of His saints, His Church. This teaching is wrong because it denies the plain teaching of Scripture that Jesus Christ *will* return *physically, bodily, and visibly* to the earth, and when He does, 'every eye will see Him,' as Revelation 1:7 says.

"As the bride of Christ, we are intimately united with Him, 'of His flesh and of His bones.' Paul addresses the same idea with the Corinthians when he writes: 'But he who is joined to the Lord is one spirit with Him,'[121] and, 'For by one Spirit we were all baptized into one body.'"[122]

"If Christ loves His bride so much," Randy said, "and if he desires so strongly to be united with her, why has He waited so long to return for her? Why didn't Jesus come back in the first century, right after He had established the Church and it had grown to millions of members?"

"There are several ways to answer your question," Eli replied. "One way is to say that it all depends on God's timing. Do you remember our earlier discussion about the 'fullness of time' and how everything that God does has a purpose?"

Randy nodded.

"Well, simply stated, Jesus did not return for His Church in the first century—and still has not returned in over 2,000 years—because the fullness of time has not come in God's plan. The time is not yet right."

"That doesn't make much sense to me," Randy said. "The longer He waits, the more people are born and die without Christ and end up in hell. What is He waiting for?"

"While it is certainly true that every day people die without Christ and go to hell. At the same time, every day new people are being brought into the kingdom of God. We have to learn to view these things from the perspective of eternity; to see them from God's viewpoint. For example, the ultimate success of God's eternal plan does not require that every human being go to Heaven. Of course it is sad—even tragic—for even one soul to go to hell, but the fact that all human beings are free moral agents makes it inevitable that some will reject God and insist on walking their own path, even into hell. To believe that God needs every human to be in Heaven requires as a logical conclusion that we believe that eventually all people will be saved. In fact, some people *do* believe that; it is a view known as *universalism.*"

"I've heard of that," Randy said, "but it goes against biblical teaching doesn't it?"

"It certainly does," Eli replied. "Jesus said, 'Enter by the narrow gate; for wide is the gate and broad is the way that leads to destruction, and there are many who go in by it. Because narrow is the gate and difficult is the way which leads to life, and there are few who find it.'[123] There are many other passages we could cite, but that one states the case as clearly as any. Not everyone will go to Heaven, and the success of God's plan does not require that they do.

"Here's another perspective on why the return of Christ may have been delayed. Have you stopped to consider the fact that 85 percent or more of all the people who have ever lived in the entire history of mankind are alive today?"

Randy shook his head. "I've never thought of it that way."

"Currently, the global population exceeds six billion, with millions more being born every day. Can you think of a *better* time for a harvest of souls to expand God's kingdom? In fact, that brings us to another perspective, one that takes us back to this fifth reason why God created man—to present to His Son a *many-membered* bride. Jesus has not returned for the simple reason that His bride, the Church, does not yet have enough members. God, in His omniscient foreknowledge, knows that the full complement of believers needed to bring the bride of Christ to completion have not yet come in. Once they have, Christ will return. But only God the Father knows exactly when this will be."

Eli pulled another book from the shelf. "I want to read to you the words of another prophet who has spent a lifetime studying and teaching on these things:

> 'Christ did not return immediately for the Early Church because it was still in its infancy and without a sufficient number of members to satisfy Him. Jesus could not be satisfied with a one-person bride as the first Adam was, because He is so full of love that it will take a Bride consisting of many millions of saints to satisfy the heart of Jesus. No one individual is capable of absorbing His love, no more than a sponge could soak up all the water in the ocean. Not even a Body of billions could exhaust the love He has for His own.

> 'Unlimited indescribable love beyond compare is flowing from the heart of Jesus to His Bride. He has been longing for the day when she will be wholly and eternally joined unto Himself. Just as a man's greatest joy is when he becomes physically one with his long-awaited bride, so the greatest joy of Jesus will be when His bride is physically resurrected and translated bodily to meet Him in the air.'[124]

"Jesus loved His bride so much, in fact, that He was willing to die and endure all sorts of pain, humiliation, and shame just to purchase her for Himself. Hebrews 12:2 says, 'looking unto Jesus, the author and finisher of our faith, who for the joy that was set before Him endured the cross, despising the shame, and has sat down at the right hand of the throne of God.'[125] What was the joy set before Jesus? The joy of purchasing His bride with His own blood and having her by His side forever.

"Even though Jesus has already purchased His bride, He will not come for her until she is prepared to meet Him. This brings us to another perspective on the delay in His return. Jesus will not return for His bride until she is fully mature and ready to take up her role as co-regent with Him in eternity. Even now He is preparing her through the Holy Spirit, and when the time is right He will come for her. Do you remember our earlier reference to Song of Solomon 4:12 where it referred to the bride as an enclosed garden, a shut-up spring and a sealed fountain? Those words relate to the question of the bride's maturity and how the bridegroom will not come for her until she is ready. The same prophet I read from a couple of minutes ago expresses this truth very well. Let him speak instead of me:

> 'The greatest longing and heart desire of Jesus is to receive His Bride, the Church, in her full perfection, beauty and maturity. He will not and cannot return for His Bride until she is complete with all necessary members, and each member and area of the body is developed to full maturity. She will be fully prepared and conformed to her Bridegroom in thought, attitude, love, power, wisdom and grace by the time He comes to receive her.

> 'Song of Solomon (also called Song of Songs) expresses the longing of the Bridegroom for the day when His Bride will be joined with Him. He is ravished with love for her and desires to be joined with His Bride, but must wait until she is fully developed. He then describes her with tingling excitement as He beholds her completeness in every area of her being. He is enthralled with her perfection of beauty and maturity.

'The Church-Bride will not be an undeveloped little sister, nor a wrinkled, blemished, or worn out old woman. When Jesus returns for His bride she will be at the peak of her beauty and performance. She will be performing greater things and be more glorious than she has been in any other generation during her existence. The perfection of beauty, maturity, ability and Christ likeness will be within her and working through her.

'When the King of kings and Lord of lords returns for His Bride, it will not be for the purpose of taking her to some celestial place in the far reaches of the universe to prepare her for her Bridehood. Christ will not return for His bride until she is ready to enter into her role as Queen of the universe because of her marriage to the King of the universe. Some speak of a three-and-a-half or seven-year honeymoon in Heaven before returning to establish earth as headquarters for a universal reign. Regardless of the honeymoon time—whether it is five seconds, three-and-a-half years, or seven years—after the honeymoon the Bride will be ushered into the throne room to sit down with Jesus at His Father's throne to begin a co-reign over God's universal domain.'"[126]

Randy had his faraway look again. "What an incredible, awesome plan! I had no idea there was so much in store for us as part of Christ's many-membered bride!"

"It is a beautiful vision, isn't it?" Eli agreed. "As Paul writes in First Corinthians, 'Eye has not seen, nor ear heard, nor have entered into the heart of man the things which God has prepared for those who love Him.'"[127]

"Eli, I know this may be a dangerous question, but is there any kind of timetable that we can identify to give us an idea of when all this will happen? I know that only God knows the exact day and hour and Jesus warned us against trying to set specific dates, but does the Bible give us any signs or clues?"

"That's a good question. You are correct in saying that we should not try to set specific dates. Many people have tried to do that in the past and they have all been wrong, obviously. However, based on certain things contained in Scripture, I think we can at least tentatively arrive at a general framework. First of all, we can consider the fact that the 'Church age,' the period from Jesus' death to His second coming, will probably be roughly 2,000 years in length. This is based on an interpretation of the dimensions of the ancient Israelite tabernacle that was constructed according to God's specific instructions. I'm talking typology here, where one thing in Scripture represents something else that comes later on. Considering the tabernacle as a type for the dispensations of time in God's plan, we can consider the total circumference of the fence around the tabernacle—1,500 linear feet—as representing the dispensation of the law. The 'Holy Place' in the tabernacle was 2,000 cubic feet in area, corresponding to 2,000 years of the Church age. The 'Holy of Holies," which was 1,000 cubic feet, represents the 1,000-year reign, or millennium, after Jesus returns.

"Using this typology, we can regard the Church age to be approximately 2,000 years long. When did the Church age begin?"

"With the death of Jesus?"

"Yes. And that took place in the year A.D. 30. Simply by adding 2,000 years we arrive at the year 2030. Remember, only God the Father knows exactly, so don't make the mistake of 'taking this to the bank' as if it is certain. This is an interpretation of typology, not Scripture.

"One way to look at the Church age is to describe it as with the growth cycle of a person. First comes the birth: A.D. 30, followed by the first great expansion under the leadership of the apostles. Next comes the junior age years, from A.D. 100-500. This was the time when the Church grew in spirit and power and nailed down its essential doctrinal positions and theology. After that came the adolescent years of falling away—what we could call the 'dark ages of the Church'—from A.D. 500-1500. The Protestant Reformation under Martin Luther and John Calvin was the second apostolic reformation of the Church and ushered in the 'teenage years' of the Church—A.D. 1500–1988.

"Every apostolic reformation has three to five major moves of God within it.[128] The third, and I believe final, apostolic reformation or restoration of the Church began in 1988 with the prophetic movement. The apostolic movement followed in 1998. I believe there will be three other movements in this final restoration of the Church: the saints movement, probably around 2008, the army of the Lord movement, around 2018, and the kingdom establishment movement, around 2028. Remember, this is just a 'framework': don't regard it as 'gospel.' There are some factors that could affect the timing, not the least of which is the Church's faithfulness or unfaithfulness in listening to and following God. If we disobey, we could end up with our own 'wilderness wandering' as the Israelites endured for 40 years."

"If what you say is accurate, that does not leave us much time to get ready."

"No, but our Lord is faithful. He will see to it that we have the time we need to prepare ourselves. We've already discussed how the bride of Christ must be mature and ready when He returns. The question is, why? Why is God restoring the Church? Why does He need or desire a restored, victorious, powerful Church going into the endtimes?"

"So that we will be ready to reign with Christ in eternity?"

"Yes, but there is more than just that. God needs one generation at the end of the ages that has come to the fullness of truth, the fullness of the life of Christ, and that possesses the wisdom, power and authority to overcome the last enemy. This enemy is so great and so strong that even though Jesus won the victory over him with His death and resurrection, no one since then has defeated him. Do you know who the final enemy is?"

"Isn't there a verse somewhere that says that death is the final enemy?"

"You are correct. Paul wrote: 'The last enemy that will be destroyed is death.'[129] How do we get victory over death? By not dying! In the final generation before the end, there will be millions of people who will leave this world and transition into immortality without going by way of the grave; what we can call the 'resurrection translation.' That is the last move of God. The final, climactic end to the last great move of God is the translation of the saints. At that point our victory will be complete. Death, the final enemy will be vanquished. The dead in Christ will rise first and we who remain will be translated with them to meet the Lord in the air.[130] Then the stage will be set for God to present His wedding present to the Bridegroom and His Bride."

"What wedding present is that?"

"An inheritance richer than any we can ever imagine here on earth. Remember what Romans 8:16-17 says? We are children of God, and if children, then…"

"Heirs of God!" Randy shouted. "And joint heirs of Christ!"

"Yes! God's wedding present to His Son and His Son's Bride— us—is to make us heirs of all that He has and is. Just as the Father has given all things to His Son, as the Bride of the Son we receive the same bequest. Because Jesus will have all things, so shall we. Revelation 21:7 says: 'He who overcomes shall inherit all things, and I will be his God and he shall be My son.'[131] Through the blood of Christ all believers are 'sons' of God regardless of gender, just as we are all the bride of Christ. By His blood we are overcomers and as overcomers we shall inherit the kingdom God has prepared for us from the foundation of the world."[132]

"With this kind of destiny ahead of us, why do so many Christians get so discouraged? I know I do at times."

"We all do, Randy, and usually it is because we lose sight of the big picture. We must practice and learn to hold onto the eternal view; to see everything from God's perspective. Discouragement comes when we get stuck on the here and now or on our circumstances of the moment. Our citizenship in the kingdom of Heaven is forever. Our membership in the Church is eternal. We are the everlasting Bride of the Son of God. Our destiny is to be conformed to the image of Christ and fulfill God's eternal purpose. As long as we maintain that focus, the trials, tests, and troubles of this life will shrink into insignificance."

7

CREATED TO BE
THE BODY OF CHRIST

After lunch, Randy and Eli continued their discussion in the parlor.

"Let's pick up where we left off," Eli said. "We were talking about the Church as the Bride of Christ, destined to be presented to Him pure and holy and without spot or blemish, ready to rule and reign with Him in the eternal realm. I have a hunch that the next reason you want to discuss regarding why God created the human race is closely related to this one. Am I right?"

"Yes," Randy replied with some surprise. "They both have to do with the Church. Before, we talked about the Church as the Bride of Christ; now I want to understand more about the Church as the Body of Christ. The two reasons are similar, but I suppose this sixth reason approaches the subject from a slightly different angle: *God created man in order to bring forth the Church as the body of Christ on earth to co-labor with Him as joint heirs in carrying out God's eternal purpose.*"

"All right, Randy," Eli said, "let me start by asking you a question: Did Jesus really want the Church?"

The question caught Randy off guard. "I'm not sure what you mean."

"Did Jesus really want the Church or was it something His Father wanted and Jesus just went along with it. Did Jesus have a personal desire for the Church?"

"Yes; of course He did."

"How do you know?"

"Well, He died for the Church when He didn't really have to. I remember the Bible saying that Jesus could have called on 10,000 angels to rescue Him from the cross and from His enemies—but He didn't. He died willingly."

"Okay, anything else?"

"The night before He was crucified, Jesus prayed for His followers. In the 17th chapter of John, Jesus prayed for His Father to protect His followers and to unite them and make them one just as He and the Father were one. That shows Jesus' desire and concern for their welfare."

"Very good. Anything else?"

"Jesus told His disciples, 'Greater love has no one than this, than to lay down one's life for his friends.'[133] Love always desires its object, and Jesus proved His love for His Church by laying down His life for it."

"Excellent, Randy. You have some very good insights. There is another proof of Jesus' desire for His Church that you have not yet mentioned, even though your other proofs have touched on it: the price Jesus paid for His Church. What did it cost Jesus to purchase the redemption of His Church?"

"His death."

"Yes, but I'm after something more specific. Let me approach it this way: What is the most precious and priceless commodity in the universe? Think along the lines of what we have been discussing over the last three days. What is of greater value than anything else?"

The inner voice in Randy's mind prompted his answer. "The blood of Christ!"

"Exactly! Nothing in all the universe is of greater value or worth than the blood of Christ, yet He gave His blood freely and without hesitation to purchase our redemption. As far as I am concerned, nothing else demonstrates better the depth of Jesus' desire for His Church. Because of the price Jesus paid, the Church is the most costly item in the universe. That which Jesus paid so much for we must take special care of. That is why Paul cautioned the leaders of the Church in Ephesus: 'Therefore take heed to yourselves and to all the flock, among which the Holy Spirit has made you overseers, to shepherd the church of God which He purchased with His own blood.'[134] Paul also said that Jesus demonstrated His love for His Church when He 'gave Himself for her' in order to 'sanctify and cleanse her' and 'present her to Himself a glorious church' without 'spot or wrinkle' and 'holy and without blemish.'"[135]

"Eli, I've noticed that there seem to be a lot of churches that don't talk about the blood of Jesus very much. Why is that?"

"In many cases it is because they either have forgotten or have never understood the importance of the blood of Jesus for the forgiveness of sin. Many churches, in the interest of modernism and political correctness, reject the message of the blood of Jesus as primitive, barbaric, and gory, and too out of touch with the sensibilities of modern man. Churches like these often reject also the historical and literal truth of the Bible, accepting its ethical and moral teachings while denying its supernatural claims. Some even go so far as to deny the historical reality of Jesus. The apostle John said that such people and 'churches'—if we can truly call them that—represent the spirit of antichrist: 'Who is a liar but he who denies that Jesus is the Christ? He is antichrist who denies the Father and the Son';[136] and 'Every spirit that does not confess that Jesus Christ has come in the flesh is not of God. And this is the spirit of the Antichrist, which you have heard was coming, and is now already in the world.'"[137]

"If the blood of Jesus is so important, how can so many churches simply dismiss it?"

"Because the enemy has blinded their eyes and darkened their minds, causing them to prefer a 'bloodless' and powerless religion that makes no costly demands on them. Paul describes such churches as 'having a form of godliness but denying its power.'[138] Satan hates

WHO AM I & WHY AM I HERE?

and fears the blood of Jesus because he knows it can save sinners and because it ensures his own destruction."

"So the blood of Christ is central to our faith as Christians."

"It is absolutely fundamental to our identity as the body of Christ. In fact, the blood of Jesus is the life of the Church. Leviticus 17:11 says that 'the life of the flesh is in the blood,' and Deuteronomy 12:23 that 'the blood is the life.' We have eternal life only because of the blood of Jesus. Without His blood we would have no life and there would be no Church. No power on earth, either natural or man-made, can match the power of Jesus' blood because His blood can transform lives. As the old gospel hymn says, 'There is power, power, wonder-working power in the precious blood of the Lamb.'

"What was it that protected the Israelites in Egypt when the death angel came and killed all the firstborn of the Egyptians?"

"Lamb's blood that they had brushed on their doorposts."

"Yes, and that lamb's blood was a type, a prefiguring that looked ahead to the eventual, once-for-all sacrifice of the Lamb of God when He poured out His blood on the cross."

"But real lamb's blood can't cleanse from sin; only Jesus' blood can. How did it work for the people of God who lived before Jesus?"

"The Israelites brought a blood sacrifice for sin as a reminder to them of the cost of atoning for their sin. Once a year on the Day of Atonement, the high priest entered the Holy of Holies in the tabernacle and, later, the temple, and offered up a sacrifice for the sins of the people. Although the blood of this sacrifice could not take away sins, it did push them forward until the day when Jesus, the Lamb of God, shed His precious blood and took those sins away in truth.

"All biblical faith looks to the cross and the shedding of Jesus' blood. The Old Testament saints looked forward in faith and time to the event that would take away their sins; the New Testament saints, and every saint of every succeeding generation have looked back in faith and time to that same event—the cross of Christ. Hebrews 9:22 says: 'According to the law almost all things are purified with blood, and without shedding of blood there is no remission.'[139] There is only one thing in all the universe that can take away our sin—the blood of Jesus.

"Unless the blood of Jesus is applied to our lives, we have no forgiveness and are still in our sins. That's what those churches who deny the blood do not understand. It doesn't matter whether our name is on a church membership roll, or whether we have been baptized in water, or how active we are in the ministries of the church; without the blood of Jesus applied to our lives, our sins remain. Again, as the old hymn says, 'What can wash away my sin? Nothing but the blood of Jesus. What can make me whole again? Nothing but the blood of Jesus. Oh! Precious is the flow that makes me white as snow. No other fount I know, nothing but the blood of Jesus.'"

"So then, all people are forgiven and saved the same way, whether they lived before or after Jesus?"

"Yes. Salvation has *always* been by grace through faith. Time is the only variable. Whether a person was looking forward in faith or backward in faith, the object of faith is the same: the Messiah, the sacrificial Lamb that God Himself would provide. That Lamb was Jesus Christ. He purchased the Church with His own blood and authorized it by His resurrection. Without Jesus' resurrection, all would have been in vain. The Church would have failed and we would all still be in our sins. But Jesus *did* rise from the dead. Through the Holy Spirit He imbued His Church with supernatural power and launched it on its destiny and purpose. Because the Church exists and is upheld by His Spirit and power, it will not fail. No matter what happens, Christ's Church will prevail and its purpose will be fulfilled."

"Sometimes that is hard to believe, considering all the disagreement and division that exist today between believers of different churches and denominations," Randy said.

"Yes. Unfortunately, that has always been a problem for the Church. The earliest Christian believers were all Jews. As the gospel spread, however, and Gentiles began to embrace the faith, the early Church faced one of its greatest challenges: overcoming centuries of prejudice and mistrust between Jews and Gentiles. Thanks to the diligent and persevering work of people like the apostles Paul and Peter, Jewish and Gentile believers came to accept each other as brothers and sisters in Christ. You remember that in our very first discussion we talked about Ephesians 2:11-18 where Paul explains that the blood of Jesus eliminates the difference between Jew and Gentile. Such unity is foundational to the very nature of the Church, not to mention its strength and growth. It is also a fruit and product of the Holy Spirit. True unity comes only from Him, and it exists among all true believers who are sensitive to the Spirit, regardless of whatever confessional or denominational label they may wear.

"Let's go back to that chapter and look at the verses that follow. Randy, read Ephesians 2:19-21."

"Now, therefore, you are no longer strangers and foreigners, but fellow citizens with the saints and members of the household of God, having been built on the foundation of the apostles and prophets, Jesus Christ Himself being the chief cornerstone, in whom the whole building, being fitted together, grows into a holy temple in the Lord, in whom you also are being built together for a dwelling place of God in the Spirit."[140]

"Remember that in the preceding verses Paul says that the blood of Christ has made all believers one and torn down the wall of separation. This essential unity is critical to understanding the nature and character of the Church as the body of Christ. In these verses you just read, what terms does Paul use to describe the Church?"

"He calls it the 'household of God,' a 'holy temple in the Lord,' and 'a dwelling place of God in the Spirit.'"

"What do those three phrases have in common?"

"They all speak of the living presence of God."

"Correct. And that is exactly what the Church is: a corporate body of individual believers who have come together as members in common and in whom, the living presence of God dwells. Now, what does Paul say about the *structure* of the Church?"

"He says that it is 'built on the foundation of the apostles and prophets' with Christ Himself as the 'chief cornerstone.'"

"What is the significance of a foundation and a chief cornerstone?"

"Well, a foundation provides support for the entire structure. That's why it has to be laid down first. As far as the other, isn't the chief cornerstone also important for supporting the structure of a building?"

"Yes. The chief cornerstone was the major structural part of ancient buildings. It had to support whatever weight was placed upon it, and its positioning guided the layout of the rest of the building. The integrity of the entire building depended upon laying a solid foundation and upon the exact placement of the chief cornerstone."

"What does Paul mean, then, when he says that the Church is built on the foundation of the apostles and prophets?" Randy asked. "I thought Christ Himself was the foundation of the Church."

"In the truest and fullest sense of the word, He is," Eli replied. "The apostles and prophets were the proclaimers of divine revelation; they gave witness to what they had both seen and heard. It is important to understand that Paul is referring to New Testament or 'Church age' prophets here rather than Old Testament prophets. What these apostles and prophets saw and heard was the Word of God, not only spoken to them but also modeled for them in the Person of Jesus Christ. He is the 'Word' as John 1:1 tells us; the ultimate self-revelation of God. By bearing faithful witness to Jesus and by accurately passing on His teachings and instructions, the apostles and prophets laid the foundation that Christ had already established.

"Tell me, Randy, on the basis of this, what does 'chief cornerstone' mean in relation to Jesus?"

"Well, just laying a solid foundation is not enough by itself; the building must be solidly constructed also. Just as the chief cornerstone supports and holds together the building, Jesus supports and holds together His Church. The full weight of the Church rests on Him, and without Him it would collapse."

"Exactly. Without Jesus the Church would collapse because without Jesus the Church has no reason to exist. Without Jesus the Church would collapse because it would be established on a false and faulty foundation. In First Corinthians 3:11, Paul himself wrote: 'For no other foundation can anyone lay than that which is laid, which is Jesus Christ.'[141]

"Now let's see what Jesus Himself had to say about the foundation of the Church. Turn to Matthew 16:13-18."

Finding the place, Randy read:

"When Jesus came into the region of Caesarea Philippi, He asked His disciples, saying, 'Who do men say that I, the Son of Man, am?' So they said, 'Some say John the Baptist, some Elijah, and others Jeremiah or one of the prophets.' He said to them, 'But who do you say that I am?' Simon Peter answered and said, 'You are the Christ, the Son of the living God.' Jesus answered and said to him, 'Blessed are you, Simon Bar-Jonah, for flesh and blood has not revealed this to you, but My Father who is in heaven. And I also say to you that you are Peter, and on this rock I will build My church, and the gates of Hades shall not prevail against it.'[142]

"I'm glad you brought up this passage, Eli," Randy said, because I have always been a little confused over it. Who or what does Jesus mean when He says, 'on this rock I will build My church'? On *what* rock? It sounds as though He is going to build His Church on Peter."

"That is what the Roman Catholic Church has maintained for centuries. They believe that Peter became the first 'bishop' of the church in Rome and therefore regard him as the first pope, from whom all other popes have descended in apostolic succession. Comparing this passage with the one in Ephesians we have already looked at, how would you answer your own question?"

"Well, Peter had just made a bold statement of faith acknowledging that Jesus was 'the Christ, the Son of the living God.' Perhaps the rock that Jesus refers to is the 'rock' of Peter's confession of faith. Peter seems to have been the leader or most prominent of the apostles, and he may have simply voiced the conclusion that all of them had reached about Jesus. The apostles were Jesus' specially chosen leaders whom He charged to preach and teach the gospel and give witness to what they had seen and heard. Since Christ Himself and His Word were at the very center of everything the apostles preached and taught, He is the true foundation upon which they built."

"Very good, Randy," Eli said. "When you let God's Word interpret itself, it's not quite as confusing is it? Let's look a little closer at Jesus' words, 'I will build My church,' because they reveal a lot about how serious Jesus is about His Church. First of all, the word 'I'; Jesus is *personally* committed to the building of His Church. 'I *will*...'; when Jesus spoke these words, the Church had not yet been birthed, but was in His sovereign will. '*Will*' indicates His determination to produce and perfect His Church regardless of the time and effort required. 'I will *build*...'; this suggests a long, slow, drawn-out process. In fact, in Ephesians 2:20, the *literal* translation of the phrase 'having been built,' is '*being built.*' 'I will build *My*...'; the Church is Jesus' personal property, pride, and possession. Christ gave Himself for it and purchased it with His own blood. 'I will build My *church*...'; Jesus' use of this word here establishes at once the distinction between this special, called-out company and every other classification of human being.[143]

"Can there be any doubt that the Church is of the utmost importance to the Lord Jesus? We are very near and dear to His heart—dear enough that He died for us. He is taking great care in building us into the body He wants us to be, a body that can carry out in His power His campaign against the enemy of God and of mankind. Notice that after Jesus says, 'I will build My church,' He says, 'and the gates of Hades shall not prevail against it.' What does that mean to you, Randy?"

"It means that the Church will stand and survive. No matter what the enemy does, he will never defeat the Church because we have the power and life of Christ in us."

"That's right, but there is more to this phrase than just the Church surviving the onslaught of the enemy. It says that the *gates* of Hades will not prevail against the Church. In this sense, these 'gates' are like the gates of the walled cities of that day that were closed to keep adversaries out. City gates were a defense against attack. With that in mind, what does this phrase say about the role of the Church as the body of Christ?"

"The Church is to do more than just stand firm against the enemy. The Church is to take the initiative; to go on the offensive, even so far as to storm the very gates of the enemy's fortress."

"Exactly. As the body of Christ, we are also a mighty army of the Lord whose mission is to take back what the enemy has stolen and to set free the millions of people he has bound in spiritual darkness. Together with them, we will grow into a living, functioning body suited for an eternal ministry and reign. We may be the body of Christ on earth, but we are also His army. We may be the bride of Christ, but under our wedding dress we are wearing combat boots."

"But what is His purpose in making us into an army? If He is all-powerful, He doesn't really *need* us to fight, does He?"

"Strictly speaking, no. But this is how He has chosen to work. It all goes back to what we have been talking about regarding God's purpose for mankind on the earth and the eternal link that we have with the earth. As with tests and trials, training and engaging in spiritual warfare build our character. The more resistance we endure and the more obstacles we overcome, the more we mature and the more prepared we are to fulfill God's purposes in our lives. We were created for dominion over the earth, and faithful service as warriors in Christ's army, His Church, helps prepare us for exercising that dominion in the eternal realm.

"There is another reason why the Lord 'needs' us as an army. Satan has enlisted millions of human beings in his service, which makes him much more dangerous than he would otherwise be. Likewise, Jesus Christ is raising up His own army of human saints to 'even the battlefield,' so to speak, and do battle with satan's human servants."

Randy's eyes opened wide in surprise. "What do you mean that satan's human servants make him more dangerous than he would be otherwise? I've never heard that before!"

"Think about it, Randy. Human beings were created for living on the earth; satan was not. Human allies make it much easier for satan to advance his agenda on earth and much harder to stop. The dynamics of a fallen world conspire with the fallen, sinful hearts of people under satan's sway to mount a formidable challenge against the kingdom of God and all who follow and serve the Lord. In the same way, Christ has raised up His own army of human allies and imbued them with His holy power so that they may defeat the enemy and break his death grip on the world."

"But I still don't understand," Randy said. "You make it sound as though human beings are stronger than satan."

"Look at it this way, Randy. Man was created in the image and likeness of God. No other creature, physical or spiritual, can make that claim; not even satan. Because we humans alone are created in God's image, we are closer to Him in nature and character than any other creature. That makes us higher than even the angels. Sin knocked us out of that high position and brought us under the control of lucifer, who was himself a fallen angel. It is only as we are restored in Christ to our former state that we once again rise to the place where, in the power of the Spirit, we are above lucifer. As the Lord's anointed army, and under His leadership and command, we, the body of Christ, can and will prevail over satan and his servants.

"This brings up an interesting point to consider. Follow me closely on this, Randy, because I want to make sure you understand what I am about to say. As you already know, God created man in His own image and likeness and gave him free will, making him a free moral agent. The qualities of man as God created him were such that if he rebelled against God he would be a *worthy opponent* for God. You might even say that this is a supplemental or corollary reason why God created man. Rebellious man as a worthy opponent would provide a good foil against which God could display His power, His majesty, His righteousness, His glory, and His holiness.

"Don't get me wrong; man is no equal to God and never will be. It's not even close. We were created to be *like* God, not to *be* God. However, as the only being in the universe created in God's image, man is closer to God than any other being and even in his fallen state makes a worthier opponent for God than does any other creature, angels included."

Eli saw the puzzled look on Randy's face. "What's the matter?" he asked.

"I understand what you're saying, Eli," Randy replied, "but I'm having trouble visualizing it. I just can't see how that could be."

"Let's see if some Scripture will help make it clearer. Look at Revelation 12:7-9."

Randy read:

"And war broke out in heaven: Michael and his angels fought with the dragon; and the dragon and his angels fought, but they did not prevail, nor was a place found for them in heaven any longer. So the great dragon was cast out, that serpent of old, called the Devil and Satan, who deceives the whole world; he was cast to the earth, and his angels were cast out with him."[144]

"Tell me, Randy, when satan and his angels rebelled in Heaven, who was dispatched to deal with the problem?"

"Michael the archangel and the angels under his command. In fact, I saw it happen; at least, I *heard* it happen when I was with Raphael before I came to see you."

"Yes. Angels were sufficient to handle the problem of fallen angels. It is different with man. Over and over throughout the Scriptures we find references to the Lord Himself fighting for His people against *human* adversaries who threaten them. Sure, you could make a case that these human adversaries were under the control and influence of satan, but they are still *human* enemies and formidable enough that the Lord fights them Himself on behalf of His people.

"Probably the clearest demonstration of this is the contest between God and Pharaoh in the Book of Exodus. Time after time God sent plagues on Egypt and time after time Pharaoh refused to let the Israelites leave the country. Finally, with the death of the Egyptian firstborn and the disaster at the Red Sea, Pharaoh was defeated. God's invincible power, awesome majesty, and eternal glory were displayed for all to see, especially the Egyptians. According to the Bible, God raised Pharaoh to his position for this very purpose. Romans 9:17 says: 'For the Scripture says to the Pharaoh, "For this very purpose I have raised you up, that I may show My power in you, and that My name may be declared in all the earth.'"

"The Book of Exodus plainly states not only that Pharaoh hardened his heart against the Lord and against Moses' demand that he free the Israelites, but also that God Himself hardened Pharaoh's heart. Read Exodus 8:32."

"But Pharaoh hardened his heart at this time also; neither would he let the people go."[145]

"Now, Exodus 9:12."

"But the Lord hardened the heart of Pharaoh; and he did not heed them, just as the Lord had spoken to Moses."[146]

"Why did God do this? Read Exodus 10:1-2."

"Now the Lord said to Moses, 'Go in to Pharaoh; for I have hardened his heart and the hearts of his servants, that I may show these signs of Mine before him, and that you may tell in the hearing of your son and your son's son the mighty things I have done in Egypt, and My signs which I have done among them, that you may know that I am the Lord.'"[147]

"Why did God harden Pharaoh's heart?"

"In order to show His signs to Pharaoh so that the Israelites would know that God was the Lord and so that they would have a legacy to pass on to their children of the great things He had done."

"That's right. God also wanted Pharaoh and the rest of the Egyptians to know and recognize that He was the Lord. The final confrontation in this contest came at the Red Sea after Pharaoh changed his mind about letting the Israelites go and, hardening his heart once more, pursued them with the intention of destroying them. This was all part of God's plan. Read Exodus 14:1-4."

"Now the Lord spoke to Moses, saying: 'Speak to the children of Israel, that they turn and camp before Pi Hahiroth, between Migdol and the sea, opposite Baal Zephon; you shall camp before it by the sea. For Pharaoh will say of the children of Israel, "They are bewildered by the land; the wilderness has

closed them in." Then I will harden Pharaoh's heart, so that he will pursue them; and I will gain honor over Pharaoh and over all his army, that the Egyptians may know that I am the Lord.' And they did so."[148]

"In this instance, what was God's purpose in hardening Pharaoh's heart?"

"So that God could gain honor over Pharaoh and his army and that the Egyptians would know that God was the Lord."

"Good. Now, skip down to verses 13 and 14. The Israelites have seen the Egyptians pursuing them and in fear have cried out to God and complained to Moses."

"And Moses said to the people, 'Do not be afraid. Stand still, and see the salvation of the Lord, which He will accomplish for you today. For the Egyptians whom you see today, you shall see again no more forever. The Lord will fight for you, and you shall hold your peace.'"[149]

"What happens next?"

"Moses stretches his staff out over the waters, the waters part and the Israelites cross the Red Sea on dry land. When the Egyptians attempt to follow, the waters come back together again and they are all drowned."

"That's right. Pharaoh is defeated and God is glorified. This is just one of the many examples in the Bible that demonstrate the fact that man in rebellion against God makes a worthy opponent against which God can display His power and glory.

"Satan has a massive army of humans ready and bound to do his bidding. In the same way, the Lord has *His* human army, an army not of slaves but of sons and daughters who serve Him willingly and freely out of love; an army of saints. This army is the Church, the body of Christ. Our purpose is to engage the enemy; to press the offensive against him in the name and power and Spirit of our Lord, who will Himself go ahead of us and lead us into battle."

"I see what you're getting at now, Eli," Randy said. "It's a new concept for me, but I'm beginning to understand. One thing has certainly become clearer to me: because the Church is Christ's army for engaging the enemy, our training is more important than ever. One reason so many Christians feel weak and experience defeat so often is that they don't really realize they are in a war with a merciless enemy. They haven't taken seriously their need for training. They assume that the Christian life is supposed to be a lark, when in reality it is a life-and-death struggle against an enemy who opposes God at every turn. I know that has been my problem in the past. Those believers who ignore their training—who neglect their maturing as disciples of Christ—will continue to experience defeat and prove of little value in the fight."

"Well spoken, Randy. You are exactly right. Whether we like it or not, as believers we are engaged in a warfare that can either make us or break us. Christ wants the struggle to *make* us—to grow us into *a* mature bride ready to reign and rule with Him. Our life on earth is the training ground for our future dominion. The Church is eternal. Our membership in the body of Christ is forever. Heaven won't be a place where we simply sit around in bliss and joy all the time. We will be engaged in meaningful work and service and ministry, just as we are supposed to be doing here.

"That is why the Lord has been so careful in birthing a Church that is just like Him. As believers, we are the 'seed' of Christ, just as Isaac, Jacob, and their descendants were the 'seed' of Abraham and became a mighty nation. Just as God begat only one Son, Jesus begat only one Church, and it includes all true believers—those of every generation and every tongue, tribe, and nation who have repented of their sins and trusted in Christ Jesus as God's promised Savior. This was God's purpose from the beginning: to bring forth on the earth a many-membered bride for His Son, a multimillions-strong corporate body of Christ who would be His physical body in the world—His hands, His feet, and His heart. As Ephesians 2:21 says, the Church was birthed to be a 'dwelling place of God in the Spirit.'"

"Why is it that so many Christians don't mature? Why do so many fail to rise to the challenge of becoming faithful, mature disciples?"

"That's a good question, with as many answers as there are people. One major reason is that many Christians simply do not believe they have anything to offer. They are ignorant of the gifts, abilities, and qualities that God has placed inside them. How many times have you heard someone say, 'I don't have any talents,' or 'I don't have any gifts,' or 'I don't have anything useful or worthwhile to contribute; how could God use me?'"

Randy smiled ruefully. "I've heard that a lot. I'm ashamed to confess that I have said something like that on more than one occasion."

"We all have, Randy, at one time or another. What we have to remember is that such thoughts are lies from the devil. As believers, all of us are gifted by God to fulfill the purpose He has for us. When we are born into the family of God through faith in Christ, we are also enlisted in Christ's army, and He will not send us into battle without equipping us for our mission. Look at Paul's words to the Corinthians. Read First Corinthians 12:4-14."

> *"There are diversities of gifts, but the same Spirit. There are differences of ministries, but the same Lord. And there are diversities of activities, but it is the same God who works all in all. But the manifestation of the Spirit is given to each one for the profit of all: for to one is given the word of wisdom through the Spirit, to another the word of knowledge through the same Spirit, to another faith by the same Spirit, to another gifts of healings by the same Spirit, to another the working of miracles, to another prophecy, to another discerning of spirits, to another different kinds of tongues, to another the interpretation of tongues. But one and the same Spirit works all these things, distributing to each one individually as He wills. For as the body is one and has many members, but all the members of that one body, being many, are one body, so also is Christ. For by one Spirit we were all baptized into one body—whether Jews or Greeks, whether slaves or free—and have all been made to drink into one Spirit. For in fact the body is not one member but many."*[150]

"One Spirit, many gifts; one body, many members, and the Spirit distributes gifts *as He wills*. In other words, we all have gifts but we do not all have the same gifts. All the gifts are important if the body of Christ is going to function properly; therefore, every member of the body is important. No matter who we are, we have a function in the body and a ministry to perform. No one is unimportant and no one is expendable. Any time any member is absent or not filling his or her special place in the body, the whole body suffers. Every member of the body of Christ is precious to Him. *Every member of the body of Christ is important.*

"Christ's purpose is to bring His body to full maturity, not only to engage the enemy in this world, but to prepare us for reigning with Him in the next. Read Ephesians 4:11-16."

> *"And He Himself gave some to be apostles, some prophets, some evangelists, and some pastors and teachers, for the equipping of the saints for the work of ministry, for the edifying of the body of Christ, till we all come to the unity of the faith and of the knowledge of the Son of God, to a perfect man, to the measure of the stature of the fullness of Christ; that we should no longer be children, tossed to and fro and carried about with every wind of doctrine, by the trickery of men, in the cunning craftiness of deceitful plotting, but, speaking the truth in love, may grow up in all things into Him who is the head—Christ—from whom the whole body, joined and knit together by what every joint supplies, according to the effective working by which every part does its share, causes growth of the body for the edifying of itself in love."*[151]

"Just as it would be a tragedy for a baby to remain a baby and never grow, so too it would be tragic for the Church that Jesus birthed to never grow to maturity. Look at all the words and phrases Paul uses to point out the importance of growth and maturity: 'edifying,' which means 'building up'; the 'fullness of Christ'; 'no longer be children'; 'grow up in all things into Him'; 'growth of the body.' For this reason, Christ gave to His Church apostles, prophets, evangelists, pastors, and teachers—the fivefold ministry. What is their purpose?"

"To equip us for ministry, to build up the body, to bring us to unity in faith and knowledge of Christ, and to mature us into the fullness of Christ—into His image and likeness."

"Good. And how does the Church grow? What makes it effective?"

"The Church grows when every member is faithful and we all work together, every member doing his or her share, exercising our gifts for each other's benefit and for the benefit of the body as a whole. In this way we build ourselves up in love and are equipped to carry out Christ's will and purpose on earth. This also prepares us for our reign and ministry in eternity."

"Excellent, Randy! There is no greater power on earth than the body of Christ working together in unity and harmony to reveal to the people of a sin-darkened world the light of Christ and the love of God that can transform them forever."

8

CREATED TO PRAISE
AND WORSHIP GOD

The sun was setting as Randy and Eli cleared away the supper dishes and settled down in the screened porch to continue their study.

"So far, Randy, we've covered six of eight reasons why God created the human race," Eli said. "Just two more and you will be ready to go home. Before we continue, however, let's review where we have come. Can you summarize for us the first six reasons?"

Randy took a deep breath and let it out slowly. "Let's see…God created man in His own image and likeness and gave him procreative power so that he could fill the earth with a whole race of beings created in God's image and likeness. God wanted a family. He also created the human race in order to make it possible for Him to take on human flesh, become one of us, and express and fulfill His love nature by dying for our sins. God created us as free moral agents so that through tests and trials we could be matured and develop a holy character in preparation for ruling with Christ in eternity.

"Another purpose for mankind in the plan of God was so that He could father His own biological Son and thus express and fulfill His own fatherly nature. Through Jesus, His only begotten Son, God also acquired the human family He desired as millions of people were born into His kingdom through faith in Christ. This also fulfilled God's original plan because all who enter His family become part of the many-membered bride of Christ, destined to rule with

Him in eternity, as well as part of the Church, the body of Christ, His mighty army commissioned to do battle with the enemy and set free those he has bound in darkness. The maturity we gain in battle also helps prepare us for our eternal ministry."

"Excellent summary, Randy. You continue to demonstrate a solid grasp of the concepts, so let's press on. The final two reasons are probably the easiest to understand because they are the most familiar to the most people. Am I right?"

"Yes," Randy replied. "Here's the first one: *God created man to offer up praise and worship to Him.*"

"That sounds pretty simple, doesn't it? Yet, there are many Christians who toss those words 'praise and worship' around without really understanding what they mean. However, if you were to ask the average Christian why God created man, probably 98 percent of them would say that we were created to praise and worship God, and they would be right. God did create us for that purpose, but as we have seen, praise and worship is only one of many reasons that God created us, and it is not even the most important reason. Let me ask you this, Randy: When did God establish praise and worship as part of man's regular relationship with Him?"

Randy looked surprised. "I've never really thought about it," he confessed. "I suppose God set it up at the very beginning, in the garden of Eden."

"Did He?" Eli raised an eyebrow. "Look back through the first three chapters of Genesis. At what point did God say, 'You are to worship Me and sing praises to Me'?"

Randy quickly scanned through the chapters in his Bible. "He didn't," Randy said with surprise in his voice. "Nowhere in this account does God say anything about praise or worship, or fellowship or prayer, for that matter."

"That's right. The creation story contains nothing about man's responsibility to offer praise and worship to God, but that does not mean it is not real. God has an unfolding revelation, an unfolding purpose for man that He reveals over time. The only instruction that God gave Adam in the garden was to *work*—to care for and keep the garden. One principle we can draw from this is that faithful, diligent, and honorable work is in itself an act of worship. We worship God whenever we set ourselves doing what He has created us to do. If we could just grasp that simple truth, we would experience so much more joy and more contentment with our circumstances."

"When did praise and worship become part of man's relationship with God?"

"Actually, Adam and Eve did both in the garden before the Fall. The Bible doesn't mention praise or worship specifically because those were completely natural parts of Adam and Eve's relationship with God. They expressed praise and worship to God in their simple, natural acknowledgment of Him as Creator and in their simple obedience to the tasks He assigned them. It was part of who they were. That part was separated, broken out, as it were, by the Fall. That which had been unforced and natural became forced and unnatural.

"Man was made for worship. God 'hard-wired' it into our being. No matter who we are, we will worship someone or something. In the garden of Eden before the Fall, man worshiped God as a natural part of his being. After the Fall, man's corrupted spirit became dulled to God's truth and subject to all kinds of ungodly influences and temptations. Consequently, man fell into worshiping all sorts of things: trees, birds, the sun, the moon, idols that he made with his own hands, even demons. If we do not worship God, we will worship something else, even ourselves, perhaps, as the 'New Age' people do who see godhood within themselves. It was not until God gave the law to Moses on Mount Sinai that the biblical command to worship God and God alone first appears.

"It was 235 years after Adam and Eve left the garden before men began to pray or to call on the name of the Lord."

"How do you know that?"

"Simple addition. Genesis 5:3-6 says that Adam was 130 years old when his son Seth was born, and Seth was 105 years old when his son Enosh was born. Genesis 4:26 says that at the time Enosh was born, men began to call on the name of the Lord."

"What happened in the meantime? Did men acknowledge God in any way? Did He receive any kind of recognition?"

"It's hard to say for sure because the Bible is silent on it. From what we can tell from Scripture, after Adam and Eve left the garden, God apparently heard nothing from man for 235 years. In fact, it appears as though God basically left man to himself for the first 1,600 years to see what they'd do with themselves. They corrupted themselves so much that He decided to destroy them with the great flood, preserving only Noah and his family who, alone of all mankind, acknowledged and called upon God.

"During all this time, the Bible makes no mention of any command or instruction to man for prayer or praise or worship; it simply is not there. When God put man in the garden He didn't tell him to cut down some trees, build a little hut, and sit there every seventh day and worship. In fact, for the first 2,500 years of man on the earth, there is no formal gathering together of the children of God, none, at least, that are recorded in Scripture. It is not until Moses receives God's instruction and revelation for building the tabernacle in the wilderness that man is for the first time told to gather together at one place to worship God. Another 500 years passed before any permanent building was set up for the worship of God: the temple that Solomon built in Jerusalem. This, according to biblical chronology, took place 3,000 years after Adam and Eve left the garden.

"Even after the birth of the Church on the Day of Pentecost, it was 200 years before believers began worshiping in buildings constructed specifically for that purpose. Until then, they met in houses or caves or grottoes—wherever they could gather safely away from official governmental persecution.

"Tell me, Randy, where in the New Testament is the Church first mentioned?"

"I'm not sure...when Jesus said, 'I will build My Church'?"

"Correct. Matthew 16:18 is the first mention of the 'church' in the New Testament. That is where we get the first indication of why Jesus really came. We know, of course, that God sent Him as the Redeemer and Savior of mankind, but it is not until He speaks of building His Church that we begin to understand His fuller purpose in coming. After all, why does Jesus save sinners? Simply so they can escape hell and go to Heaven? What do you think?"

"Well, saving us from hell is certainly part of the deal, but I know from our talks these past three days that there is a lot more involved. Jesus saves sinners so that He can have a bride and a body on earth to carry out His will and mission. He saves sinners so that His Father can have a great, eternal, human family. Isn't this what Paul meant when he wrote that God was in Christ reconciling the world to Himself?"[152]

"It is indeed. Very good, Randy. Christ instituted the Church, and although structurally it focused on small, local bodies from the very beginning, Christ has always had a universal, global scope in mind. So often we get caught up in our own local churches and our own ideas and preferences for music and worship styles that we tend to forget the global scope of God's purpose. We need to recapture His vision for the Church; a much bigger vision than most of us have because He envisions the world. His unfolding revelation has brought us to the place where we need to understand that the mission of the Church is more than just building new local churches with a local focus; our mission is to establish the kingdom of God on the earth. Our vision and our goal must be global in scope because that matches our Lord's vision and goal. We must have a world view.

"God's original command to Adam and Eve was to be fruitful, multiply, and fill the earth. That same command applies to the Church. Multiplication is a biblical principle. Do you remember Jesus' parable of the talents?"

"Yes. A man who was leaving on a journey gave money to three of his servants; one talent to one, two talents to another, and five talents to the third. The servants with five and two talents invested their money and doubled it in returns. The servant with one talent simply buried it for safekeeping and awaited his master's return. When the master returned, he praised the first two servants for their faithfulness and their fruitfulness in multiplying what he had given them. He punished the third servant, however, and took away the talent he had given him and gave it to the servant who now had ten talents. To the two faithful servants he said, 'Well done, good and faithful servant; you were faithful over a few things, I will make you ruler over many things. Enter into the joy of your lord.'"[153]

"That's right. In the same way, Christ's desire and expectation of His Church is that we multiply and increase, filling the earth with children of God drawn from every tongue, tribe, and nation. This is the vision behind Jesus' command: 'Go therefore and make disciples of all the nations, baptizing them in the name of the Father and of the Son and of the Holy Spirit, teaching them to observe all things that I have commanded you; and lo, I am with you always, even to the end of the age.'[154]

"If God gives you one talent, and you give it back to Him with no addition, will He be satisfied? No. He expects multiplication. His command to us is, 'Multiply; grow in the grace and knowledge and wisdom of God, and in the nature and character of Christ; add new saints to the kingdom, and fill the earth with them.'

"So, even though the Church was in God's heart and mind and plan from the very beginning, His revelation to men of the Church as the people of God was of an unfolding nature. As far as we know from Scripture, for the first 2,500 years of man's existence there was no command from God—no divine directive—for praise and worship. It is really not until David comes along, the man 'after God's own heart' that we get the revelation of praise and worship as a service we are to offer to God. The Psalms are filled with calls to praise and worship God. In fact, the Bible as a whole contains over 900 verses dealing with worship, praise, joy, rejoicing, music, song, and singing, but the vast majority of them do not appear until at least the time of Moses, and many of them, the time of David and after. Prior to Moses, there are perhaps ten verses relating to praise or worship, but they are merely references and not commands.

"For example, the phrase 'praise the Lord' appears only 55 times in the Old Testament. Except for one instance in the 29th chapter of Genesis related to the birth Jacob's son Judah, the phrase does not appear until First Chronicles 6:4: 'And [David] appointed some of the Levites to minister before the ark of the Lord, to commemorate, to thank, and to praise the Lord God of Israel.' Of those

55 occurrences, 35 of them are in the Psalms. In contrast, the phrase, 'praise God' occurs only once—in Psalm 150:1. The word 'worship' appears 117 times in the Old Testament, but its first occurrence is as late as the 22nd chapter of Genesis, in relation to Abraham's offering of Isaac.

"All in all, the Bible contains over 500 verses that *specifically* exhort man to worship, magnify, praise, and glorify God. Such is also our duty, responsibility, and privilege. Praise and worship of God are appropriate and proper activities for us as His children, but the scriptural instruction to do so is a revelation of unfolding nature."

"One thing puzzles me, Eli," Randy said. "The Bible talks about angels in Heaven that continually praise and worship God. With all the millions of angels surrounding Him and offering up praise to Him, why does God need or desire *our* praise and worship? What can our praise and worship do for God or give Him that the praise and worship of the angels cannot?"

"Good question, Randy. Part of the answer goes back to our discussion about the love nature of God. Why wasn't God's love nature satisfied by the creation of the angels?"

"Because He wanted to love and be loved by creatures who were like Him—beings who were created in His own image and likeness."

"That's right, and the same idea applies to praise and worship."

"Oh, I see what you mean! The angels worship God and offer Him praise, but they are not created in His image. God desires praise and worship from us because we are created in His image. We are more like God than is any other creature."

"Exactly. There is another reason as well, and it also relates to the difference between man and the angels. Aside from being created in God's image and likeness, what else makes us different from the angels?"

"Our ability to procreate?"

"That is a difference, yes, but I'm looking for something more basic. Let me rephrase the question. What makes us different from satan and the rest of the fallen angels?"

"We are redeemable and they are not."

"Absolutely right. Because we know not only the reality of lostness and separation from God due to sin, but also the joy of redemption and reconciliation with God in Christ, our praise and worship carry a quality of joy, appreciation, and thankfulness that the praise and worship of the angels in Heaven do not. Peter describes the mysteries of the gospel and the saving grace of God toward men as 'things which angels desire to look into.'[155] Since the angels that are still in Heaven have never known what it is like to be lost, neither do they know what it is like to be redeemed and restored. Salvation is a dimension that is completely alien to them."

"So what you're saying is that our praise and worship is especially important to God not only because we are like Him in nature, but because as redeemed creatures we see and know His greatness and love and mercy in a way no other creature does."

"Yes. We praise and worship God freely because He has redeemed us and we know that no one else is worthy of our worship. And that brings up another issue. Why does God hate idolatry?"

"Because of who He is. The Bible says that He is a jealous God; jealous for His name and glory and honor."

"That's right. Isaiah 42:8 says, 'I am the Lord, that is My name; and My glory I will not give to another, nor My praise to carved images.' Yes, God hates idolatry because of who He is, but that's not all. He also hates idolatry because of who we are."

"What do you mean?"

"Man was created in the image and likeness of God. Of all God's created order, we alone bear that distinction. That makes us unique. It also means that man is the apex, the crowning glory of God's creativity. In all of creation, nothing is higher than man. Of course, as Creator, God is infinitely higher than we are. Worship involves venerating something or someone that is higher than ourselves. God alone is worthy of our worship and praise because He alone is higher than we are. God hates idolatry because it raises a creature into the place of the Creator and usurps God's rightful place. Idolatry also diminishes *man* because we take something that is *lower* than we are and elevate it into something *higher* than we are. As long as we worship the creature rather than the Creator, we will be alienated from God. As long as we venerate something lower than we are as being higher than we are, we will fail to rise to the place for which God created us. We will never reach our potential or fulfill our destiny in God's plan."

"Oh, I see your point now. I've never thought about idolatry that way."

"It really changes your outlook. Once you understand that idolatry not only offends God but also diminishes you, you will be more sensitive to things other than God that you tend to allow to have first place in your life.

"Let's turn now to a biblical example of praise and worship in action. Read Revelation 4:1-11."

Randy read:

"After these things I looked, and behold, a door standing open in heaven. And the first voice which I heard was like a trumpet speaking with me, saying, 'Come up here, and I will show you things which must take place after this.' Immediately I was in the Spirit; and behold, a throne set in heaven, and One sat on the throne. And He who sat there was like a jasper and a sardius stone in appearance; and there was a rainbow around the throne, in appearance like an emerald. Around the throne were twenty-four thrones, and on the thrones I saw twenty-four elders sitting, clothed in white robes; and they had crowns of gold on their heads. And from the throne proceeded lightnings, thunderings, and voices. Seven lamps of fire were burning before the throne, which are the seven Spirits of God. Before the throne there was a sea of glass, like crystal. And in the midst of the throne, and around the throne, were four living creatures full of eyes in front and in back. The first living creature was like a lion, the second living creature like a calf, the third living creature had a face like a man, and the fourth living creature was like a flying eagle. The four living creatures, each having six wings, were full of eyes around and within. And they do not rest day or night, saying: 'Holy, holy, holy, Lord God Almighty, Who was

and is and is to come!' Whenever the living creatures give glory and honor and thanks to Him who sits on the throne, who lives forever and ever, the twenty-four elders fall down before Him who sits on the throne and worship Him who lives forever and ever, and cast their crowns before the throne, saying: 'You are worthy, O Lord, to receive glory and honor and power; for You created all things, and by Your will they exist and were cre-ated.'"[156]

"Here's the scenario: John, in a vision, has been invited up to Heaven, and he describes the cast of characters that play out the scene before him. First, there is the Lord, sitting on a throne, then 24 elders sitting on 24 thrones around the Lord's throne, and finally, 4 living creatures surrounding the Lord's throne. Who are the 24 elders?"

"I've heard somewhere that they probably represent the 12 tribes of Israel and the 12 apostles of Jesus."

"You are very likely correct, even though John never clearly identifies them. If they do represent the tribes of Israel and the apostles, then this is a symbolic picture of all the saints of God—the Old Testament 'Church' and the New Testament Church—reigning and ruling in eternity. Who are the four living creatures?"

"From John's description, they sound like angels. Their appearance is very similar to what Isaiah describes in his vision in Isaiah chapter six."

"Yes. More specifically, they are seraphim; one was like a lion, another like a calf, a third with a face like a man, and the fourth like an eagle. Some scholars and commentators link these creatures with the four Gospel writers, Matthew, Mark, Luke and John, as well as the four standard-bearers of the children of Israel when they were encamped around the tabernacle. Each standard had its own flag with its own picture: a lion, a calf, a man, and an eagle. When John sees the four living creatures, what are they doing?"

"They are praising God."

"And how long have they been praising God?"

"I don't know...a long time, probably. Maybe ever since they were created. Isn't the praise of God around His throne the continual activity of some of the angels? I witnessed similar activity when I entered Heaven's throne room with Raphael."

"I'm sure you did, Randy, and you are quite correct. The Bible says that the hosts of Heaven do offer up constant praise and worship to the Most High God. This vision of the four living creatures has particular significance."

"How so?"

"Psalm 22:3 says, 'But You are holy, enthroned in the praises of Israel.' Another way to express this is to say that God *inhabits* the praises of His people. The praises of God's people draw His presence and His presence brings His power. God's presence and power permeate the universe and hold everything together. By their continual praises, the four living creatures that John describes are like Heaven's 'power generators.' Their praises 'pull in' the presence of God and release the power of God, just like a power generator on earth. When we praise God here on earth, we draw in His presence and release His power. If we want to be 'power producers,' we must be praisers and worshipers.

"The four living creatures say, 'Holy, holy, holy, Lord God Almighty, who was and is and is to come!' With these words they are extolling God's holiness, Lordship, and eternal nature. Their praise inspires the 24 elders to fall before the Lord's throne, cast their crowns at His feet, and worship Him, saying, 'You are worthy, O Lord, to receive glory and honor and power; for You created all things, and by Your will they exist and were created.' The praises of the 24 elders extol God's *worthiness* to receive all praise. By extolling His creativity, they praise Him for His omniscience, His omnipotence, and His omnipresence.

"In the same way, the Lord inhabits our praises. When we praise and worship God with our whole heart and a right spirit, we draw into His presence and release His power. Our praise can be verbal, but it is more than verbal. The Bible tells us to love God with all our heart, soul, mind, and strength. That goes far beyond simply the words we say. In Ephesians 1:12, Paul writes, 'We who first trusted in

Christ should be to the praise of His glory.'[157] What did we say His glory in us is?"

"Being conformed to the image of Christ."

"That's right. Praising God with our lips as well as our lives helps mold us into Christ's image because that is what He did. Everything Jesus said and did was an act of worship in praise of His Father. As we learn to practice consistent praise, we are gradually transformed from glory to glory until we come into the very image and likeness of Christ. None of us will achieve that fully in this life, but we can work toward it. That process will be completed when we pass into glory either at our death or at our translation when Jesus returns. In the meantime, we are called to praise His character, His nature, His life, who He is, what He is, and what He does. Our lives should extol, magnify and demonstrate the character of Jesus, always offering praise to His glory."

"I had always thought of praise primarily as something verbal; something that I offered with my lips."

"It is. Praise is verbal, but as I said before, it is more than just that. Verbal praise that is not backed up by a consistent life of praise does not count for much. The old proverb 'actions speak louder than words' is very true in our spiritual lives. Our lifestyle must agree with our words or our words are meaningless. Read Hebrews 13:15-16."

"Therefore by Him let us continually offer the sacrifice of praise to God, that is, the fruit of our lips, giving thanks to His name. But do not forget to do good and to share, for with such sacrifices God is well pleased."[158]

"Notice that verse 15 speaks not only of 'praise,' but of a 'sacrifice of praise.' What is that sacrifice of praise?"

"The 'fruit of our lips, giving thanks to [God].'"

"In other words, *verbal* praise. But in the next verse our verbal praise is linked to a lifestyle of praise when we are told to 'do good and to share.' These too are 'sacrifices' with which God is pleased."

"Okay, we've talked about the kind of praise that pleases God, but what kind of worship pleases God? So many churches worship so many different ways. How can we know what pleases God and what doesn't?"

"That is an excellent question, Randy. If more churches took the time to ask—and to answer—that question, there would be fewer of them that have 'dead' worship. The key to live and dynamic worship is not so much *style* as it is *heart*. God always looks at the heart. He is more interested in who we *are* than in what we *do*. The attitude of our heart in worship is of far greater importance to God than the style in which we worship. Jesus got into a discussion with a Samaritan woman over this very issue. Read John 4:20-24."

> "'Our fathers worshiped on this mountain, and you Jews say that in Jerusalem is the place where one ought to worship.' Jesus said to her, 'Woman, believe Me, the hour is coming when you will neither on this mountain, nor in Jerusalem, worship the Father. You worship what you do not know; we know what we worship, for salvation is of the Jews. But the hour is coming, and now is, when the true worshipers will worship the Father in spirit and truth; for the Father is seeking such to worship Him. God is Spirit, and those who worship Him must worship in spirit and truth.'"[159]

"What do you think, Randy? What was the basic problem with this woman's idea of worship?"

"She thought that proper worship depended on a particular place, such as on a mountain in Samaria, just as the Jews said it should be in Jerusalem."

"That's right; and Jesus corrected both errors. He said that the *place* of worship is not particularly important because places are temporary. The day will come when those places are no more. Instead, He said, the important thing about worship is the attitude of the worshiper. What kind of worshiper does God seek?"

"Those who worship Him in 'spirit and truth.' I've always wondered exactly what that means."

"It means that worship is more than outward actions or ritual. Worship is an attitude of the heart; an inclination of our inmost being. Our worship must be spiritual worship and it must be truthful worship. John 1:17 says that 'grace and truth came through Jesus Christ.' Jesus said, 'I am the way, the truth, and the life.'[160] Paul told the Romans, 'I beseech you therefore, brethren, by the mercies of God, that you present your bodies a living sacrifice, holy, acceptable to God, which is your reasonable service.'[161] Here we have the word *sacrifice* again, and once again a lifestyle of sacrifice is in view. The phrase 'your reasonable service' can also be translated, 'your spiritual service of worship.'[162]

"When Jesus says we must worship 'in spirit and truth' He is saying we must worship with our whole being and that our worship must be based on truth, which is found in Him. Worship that is acceptable to God is worship that is in the Spirit of Christ and in the truth of Christ.

"But back to your original question, Randy. You asked what God gets from our praise and worship that He does not get from the praise and worship of the angels. I would have to say that the answer is *intimacy*. Because God is our Father and we are His children, He desires intimate fellowship and interaction with us. Our praise and worship draw us into His presence and opens the way for that intimate fellowship. God's desire is to restore us to the kind of intimacy with Himself that Adam and Eve enjoyed before the Fall. Why does God seek that kind of intimacy with man and not with the angels?"

"Because man is created in the image and likeness of God and the angels are not."

"Exactly. Because we were created to be like God in nature and character, we can relate to Him in an intimate and personal way that the angels cannot. We are God's children; the angels are not. We are God's family; the angels are not. We are the bride of Christ; the angels are not. Children, family, bride; all of these terms imply intimacy.

"God wants us to praise and worship Him from a free and willing heart not only because He desires intimate fellowship with us but also because He designed us that way. God created us for praise and worship and if we do not worship God we will worship someone or something else, because that's the way we are wired. God wants our praise and worship not only because He deserves it but also because He knows that we will never be fully fulfilled in our lives until we are doing what we were designed to do.

"God has no ego to satisfy. He does not *need* our praise and worship but He knows that we need it. Praising and worshiping God is more for our benefit than for God's. We were created to be like Christ and to be conformed to His image and likeness. This means we have to know Him. The best way to know someone is through regular intimate contact. Understand that by 'intimate contact' I mean close, transparent, vulnerable, and personal contact."

"In the end then," Randy said, "this reason for God creating man is connected with all the others. God created us to praise and worship Him so that He could have intimate fellowship with us and we with Him. God's desire for intimacy with us is related to His love, His Fatherhood, and His desire for a great human family. The more intimate we are with Him the more like Him we become, which is also one of the reasons He created us."

"You are absolutely right, Randy. All of God's reasons for creating mankind are related to each other because they all issue forth from God's heart. Praise and worship helps us become more intimate with God and intimacy, over time, produces Christlikeness in mind, heart, and character. Christlikeness prepares us for our destiny as co-rulers with Christ over His eternal realm. It is all connected.

"I think that is enough for this session. Tomorrow we will deal with the final reason for God creating man, and then you will be ready to return home."

9

CREATED FOR FELLOWSHIP WITH GOD

Randy woke at dawn the next morning after the most restful sleep he had ever had. As first light spread across the eastern sky, he rose and gazed out the window, watching as once again the mist rose from the ground to water the earth as far as he could see. A surge of excitement filled his heart as he realized that his time with Eli was drawing to a close and he would be going home soon. At the same time, he felt a twinge of regret.

Despite his desire to return home, Randy also was reluctant to leave. Even though he had only been here a few days, his heart felt completely at peace in this place. His spirit had been refreshed and nourished as never before and a big part of him wanted to stay. *I suppose this is how Peter, James, and John must have felt when they were with Jesus on the Mount of Transfiguration,* Randy thought. *They didn't want to leave, either.*

Randy stood silently at the window for a long time, rapt in his thoughts and the wonder of the Eden-like world coming to light before him once again under the rays of the rising sun. Finally, the aroma of breakfast cooking caught his attention and he walked into the kitchen to help Eli prepare their morning meal.

After breakfast Randy and Eli, Bibles in hand, sat down on the bench at the back of the apple orchard for their final session together.

"Well Randy," Eli began, "we've covered a lot of ground over the last few days, but the end is in sight. How do you feel about everything we've talked about? Do you understand everything? Is there anything you still have questions about?"

"Actually, no," Randy answered. "Everything is pretty clear to me. I will say that when I started I had no idea of the depth and complexity behind the creation of man. To be perfectly honest, I never gave it much thought. I simply accepted the teachings I received at church and never even considered digging more deeply into the subject. Having learned the eight reasons why God created the human race, however, I am already discovering that the Bible as a whole is starting to make more sense to me. Now that I have a better understanding of God's purposes for man, I'm finding that I can see those purposes being played out in Scripture where I couldn't see them before."

Eli nodded and smiled. "Good. I'm glad this time has been helpful for you. We have one final reason to discuss but before we start, let's recap one final time to see where we've come. What is the first reason why God created man?"

"God created man to fill the earth with beings in the image and likeness of Himself."

"Good. And number two?"

"God created man to reveal His own heart and nature as Love by dying for us. Before He could do that, He needed the human race so that He could take on a physical body and become one of us."

"Fine. Number three?"

"God created man with free moral agency. He endowed us with free moral choice so that we could be tested, tried, and purified in every realm of living, being, and doing. His ultimate purpose is to conform us to the image of Christ and prepare us to reign with Him."

"Okay; what about number four?"

"God created the human race with the power of procreation so that He could father a genetic, biological Son rather than just a created Son. Adam was a created son but Jesus was the actual, biological, begotten Son of God, who was conceived by the Holy Spirit and born of the virgin Mary. By this means, God fulfilled His nature as an everlasting Father."

"Great; and number five?"

"God created the human race in order to provide a many-membered bride for His Son. The love of Christ is so deep and unfathomable, and so unbelievably extensive that only a bride consisting of millions of human beings could even begin to absorb it and return enough love to Him to fill His heart. As the bride of Christ, we are being prepared for our role of reigning with Him in eternity."

"Very good. Number six?"

"God created man in order to bring about the Church, which is not only the bride of Christ, but the body of Christ on earth. Whereas the bride speaks more of our relationship with Christ as well as our ruling with Him in eternity, the Church is the expression of Christ's body on earth, called to co-labor with Him as joint heirs and as an army under His command to go on the offensive against the enemy. Although birthed at a specific point in time, the Church is eternal. Our service and ministry will continue on beyond this life."

"All right; and number seven?"

"God created man to offer praise and worship to Him. He alone is worthy of our praise and worship because He alone is higher than we are. When we worship someone or something other than God we diminish not only God, who alone deserves our worship, but ourselves as well because we take something that is lower than we are and elevate it to a place higher than we are."

"Excellent. And finally, we come to reason number eight, which is?"

"God created man for fellowship with Him."

"Okay, let's start there. What does the word *fellowship* mean to you?"

"I think of fellowship as getting together with friends or family for talk and fun and recreation. Fellowship to me is interaction and communication with other people, particularly those whom I love and am closest to."

"You have a good general understanding already of what fellowship means. How does that translate to our relationship with the Lord? What does it mean to have fellowship with God?"

"I think it means spending time with Him and talking to Him in prayer and listening to Him talk to me through the Holy Spirit and through His Word, the Bible."

"You're absolutely right, Randy. There are too many Christians who never enjoy full fellowship with God because they have a shallow or insufficient understanding not only of what fellowship with God *is*, but also what it *involves*. Let's see if we can deepen *our* understanding by examining what the Word of God says about fellowship. First of all, let's look at Acts 2:42."

Randy read:

"And they continued steadfastly in the apostles' doctrine and fellowship, in the breaking of bread, and in prayers."[163]

"Notice, Randy, that this verse contains all the activities you mentioned as defining fellowship: Scripture, or the 'apostles' doctrine, interaction with other people, or 'breaking of bread,' and prayer. This verse is the first occurrence in the New Testament of the word *fellowship*. The Greek word is *koinonia*, which means 'partnership,' or 'participation.' *Koinonia* also carries the idea of communion and communication. Thus, *koinonia*, or biblical fellowship, involves something much deeper and more intimate than simple social interaction. People can gather together for social activities and fun and never have more than surface contact with each other. True *koinonia* penetrates below the surface and draws people into heart-to-heart communion and interaction both with each other and with God. Read First Corinthians 1:9."

"God is faithful, by whom you were called into the fellowship of His Son, Jesus Christ our Lord."[164]

"Acts 2:42 mentioned fellowship between believers in the Church. This verse speaks of our fellowship with Christ. The two go together. Although we each have fellowship individually with Christ, the only way to keep that fellowship strong is by regular fellowship with other believers in the context of a local church. Christ saves us individually, but He never intends for us to be individualistic. As we discussed earlier concerning the body of Christ, we all need each other. The body is not complete unless every member is in place. Look now at Galatians 2:9."

"And when James, Cephas, and John, who seemed to be pillars, perceived the grace that had been given to me, they gave me and Barnabas the right hand of fellowship, that we should go to the Gentiles and they to the circumcised."[165]

"Randy, what does Paul mean when he says that James, Cephas (or Peter), and John gave he and Barnabas the 'right hand of fellowship'?"

"He means that Peter, James, and John accepted the mission of Paul and Barnabas to carry the gospel to the Gentiles as being equally legitimate and God-ordained as their own calling to preach the gospel to the Jews."

"Exactly. Involvement in a common cause fosters fellowship. Unfortunately, so often today Christians of different groups or denominations get so caught up in their differences that instead of extending the right hand of fellowship, they offer the 'left foot' of fellowship. Biblical *koinonia* involves embracing our common bond in Christ while at the same time acknowledging our legitimate differences. Another way to say this is 'unity in diversity.'"

"What about people in cults or in groups like the Mormons or the Jehovah's Witnesses?"

"*True* biblical *koinonia* is possible only between people who share a common belief that Jesus Christ is the divine Son of God and who have been born again of the Spirit of God into eternal life through the forgiveness of their sins. People outside this parameter of faith, no matter what group they associate with, are not in true fellowship with us because they are not in true fellowship with our Lord. At times we may associate with them on social or even religious occasions, but we cannot truly say that we are in *koinonia* with them or them with us. Read Philippians 2:1-2."

> *"Therefore if there is any consolation in Christ, if any comfort of love, if any fellowship of the Spirit, if any affection and mercy, fulfill my joy by being like-minded, having the same love, being of one accord, of one mind."*[166]

"Actually, these two verses describe the characteristics of true 'fellowship of the Spirit': consolation in Christ, comfort of love, affection, mercy, and like-mindedness. Those qualities abound when true koinonia is present. Look at Philippians 3:10."

> *"That I may know Him and the power of His resurrection, and the fellowship of His sufferings, being conformed to His death."*[167]

"Paul speaks here of sharing the 'fellowship' of Christ's sufferings. What do you think that means?"

"I think Paul means that he wanted to identify completely with Christ, not just in the good things of grace and mercy and salvation, but also in the bad things, such as Christ's suffering on the cross. Paul felt that he could not rightfully enjoy one without embracing the other."

"That's a very astute observation, Randy. Too many Christians today act as if Christianity is nothing more than a 'bless me' club that exists to give them comfort and bliss and prosperity. In truth, God is more interested in making us righteous than in making us comfortable. One of the purposes of our fellowship with Christ is to make us righteous like Him, but that involves our willingness to identify with Christ in every way, including His suffering. Being a Christian means enjoying the peace and presence and prosperity of Christ, but it also means denying ourselves, taking up our cross daily and following Him.[168]

"There's an old hymn that says, 'Draw me nearer, nearer, blessed Lord, to the cross where Thou hast died; draw me nearer, nearer,

nearer, blessed Lord, to Thy precious bleeding side.' How often have we sung those words without giving any thought to what they really mean? To be drawn nearer to the cross and nearer to Jesus' bleeding side is a request to be brought into closer identity with His suffering, and many Christians are not willing to do that. Unless we are willing to embrace Jesus' suffering—persecuted by man, forsaken by God, shamed, humiliated, and ridiculed—our fellowship with Him will never be as full or deep or rich as it could be.

"The apostle John's first letter has a lot to say about fellowship. Let's go there now. Randy, read First John 1:3-7."

"That which we have seen and heard we declare to you, that you also may have fellowship with us; and truly our fellowship is with the Father and with His Son Jesus Christ. And these things we write to you that your joy may be full. This is the message which we have heard from Him and declare to you, that God is light and in Him is no darkness at all. If we say that we have fellowship with Him, and walk in darkness, we lie and do not practice the truth. But if we walk in the light as He is in the light, we have fellowship with one another, and the blood of Jesus Christ His Son cleanses us from all sin."[169]

"According to John, who do we have fellowship with?"

"With other believers, but also with God the Father and with Christ Himself."

"That is another example of why it is important for Christians to practice fellowship with one another. The more we fellowship together as brothers and sisters in Christ, the more we experience fellowship with God. Our own individual fellowship is strengthened and enhanced when we come together as the Church in corporate fellowship. Remember the words of Jesus: 'For where two or three are gathered together in My name, I am there in the midst of them.'[170]

"What metaphor does John use as an equivalent for fellowship?"

"To 'walk in the light'?"

"Yes. What two benefits come to us by walking in the light?"

"We have fellowship with one another and the blood of Jesus cleanses us from our sin."

"That's right. If you are walking, the only people you can have fellowship with are others who are walking the same direction you are. That's why we cannot have true biblical fellowship with non-believers or with cults or other groups that do not preach or teach the true gospel; they are not walking the same way we are. They are walking in darkness. Jesus walks in the light, so if we walk in the light, that means we are walking with Jesus, and in His company, our sins are washed away."

"Verse seven says that *if* we walk in the light, the blood of Jesus cleanses us from sin. What if we stop walking in the light, as in back-sliding? Does the blood of Jesus stop cleansing us?"

"That's a very interesting question, Randy. In the Greek, the verb form is that of continuing action. Literally, it says that if we walk *continually* in the light, the blood of Jesus *continually* cleanses us of our sin. When we are born again by the Spirit of God, the blood of Jesus washes away our sin and we are forgiven, and that is a *permanent* transaction. As long as we walk in the light, or walk with Christ, His presence and power in our lives help us experience victory day by day. If we backslide or turn aside from walking faithfully in the light, we are still saved, but we are no longer under His protecting and covering power. We become more prone to satan's deception, which leads more and more to spiritual defeat. That is why walking in the light consistently is so very important.

"Since we're talking about walking in the light, this would be a good time to discuss fellowship from a slightly different angle: fellowship as *walking with God.* Throughout the Bible, walking with God is a common metaphor for fellowship with Him. The Bible speaks often of people who walked with God. Who was the first to do so?"

Randy thought for a few moments, and then said, "Wasn't it Enoch?"

"True, Enoch is the first person the Bible specifically states as walking with God, but I believe Adam and Eve did, too, at least before the Fall. Look at Genesis 3:8."

"And they heard the sound of the Lord God walking in the garden in the cool of the day, and Adam and his wife hid themselves from the presence of the Lord God among the trees of the garden."[171]

"This, of course, is immediately after Adam and Eve have disobeyed God by eating the fruit from the tree of the knowledge of good and evil. The verse speaks of God 'walking in the garden in the cool of the day' and of Adam and Eve hiding from Him. Although nothing is explicitly stated, I believe the implication is that walking in the garden was a regular activity for God and that it was customary, until this day, for Adam and Eve to join Him. This was part of their ongoing fellowship with God. Their absence on this occasion prompted God's question to Adam in the next verse: 'Where are you?' Tell me, Randy, why would God ask such a question? Isn't He omniscient? Didn't He know where Adam was?"

"God's question was not because He did not know, but to draw Adam into acknowledging what he had done. It was God's way of confronting them with their sin and forcing them to face the reality of it."

"That's right. Fellowship with God means walking with God—walking in the light. Until that day, Adam and Eve walked in the light. They walked with God and He was their life, their light, and their joy. As soon as they ate of the forbidden fruit, they turned from the light and began walking in darkness. They were no longer walking with God and He had to seek them out.

"After the Fall and prior to the days of Noah, only one person is described in the Bible as walking with God, and that was Enoch, as you said before. Genesis 5:24 says simply: 'And Enoch walked with God; and he was not, for God took him.'[172] Hebrews 11:5 adds that Enoch's testimony was that he 'pleased God.' How did Enoch please God?"

"By walking with God."

"That's right. And the Bible calls that *faith*: 'But without faith it is impossible to please Him, for he who comes to God must believe that He is, and that He is a rewarder of those who diligently seek Him.'[173] Faith and walking with God go hand-in-hand. It is impossible to walk with God without faith in Him. On the other hand, faith that does not result in walking with God is an extremely weak faith that is practically worthless."

"I want to walk with God," Randy said, "and I believe I am for the most part, but sometimes I'm not sure that I fully understand *how* to walk with Him."

"Well, regular Bible study and prayer, like we talked about earlier, are very important. Sometimes, using different terminologies can help in our understanding. Walking with God can also be called 'walking by faith,'[174] 'walking in truth,'[175] 'walking in love,'[176] and 'walking in the Spirit.'[177] It means learning to live a life of complete dependence upon God rather than on ourselves. Walking in the Spirit is the opposite of walking in the flesh.

"Walking *with* God means going in the same direction He is going, keeping in step with Him, walking neither ahead of Him nor behind Him, but staying with Him. When we walk with God at His pace we are in a position to communicate with him and him with us. How can we hear God if we are constantly running ahead or lagging behind, or wandering off onto every little bypath that comes along?

"All right; Adam and Eve walked with God before the Fall, and Enoch walked with God after the Fall. Who is the next person who walked with God?"

"Noah?"

"Correct. Read Genesis 6:5-9."

"Then the Lord saw that the wickedness of man was great in the earth, and that every intent of the thoughts of his heart was only evil continually. And the Lord was sorry that He had made man on the earth, and He was grieved in His heart. So the Lord said, 'I will destroy man whom I have created from the face of the earth, both man and beast, creeping thing and birds of the air, for I am sorry that I have made them.' But Noah found grace in the

eyes of the Lord. This is the genealogy of Noah. Noah was a just man, perfect in his generations. Noah walked with God."[178]

"I wanted you to read all those verses so you could contrast Noah's walk with God with the conditions of the world in which he lived. We think our world is bad and tough to live in as Christians; imagine what it was like for Noah, trying to live righteously in a world where 'every intent of the thoughts of [man's] heart was only evil continually.' Noah's world was filled with wickedness and evil, but Noah himself was just and 'perfect in his generations.' Being 'just' and 'perfect' is another way of describing what it means to walk with God."

"Looking at it that way, Eli, puts us all to shame. I mean, if Noah could be just and perfect in his generation even in the midst of a totally evil and corrupt world, what excuse do we have for not doing the same in our own world?"

"You're absolutely right, Randy. What excuse do we have? After all, living on this side of the cross and the resurrection and Pentecost, we have many advantages and benefits that Noah and other ancient men and women of God did not have. We have the Holy Spirit living in us continually and the living Christ interceding for us unceasingly before the throne of His Father.[179] We have the gifts of the Spirit to equip us to live for Him and do His will. We have the witness in Scripture of those men who knew Jesus better than anyone else: Peter, James, John, Matthew, and the other apostles who spent three and a half years in His constant company, as well as Paul who, although not one of the original 12, received a powerful vision of the living Christ and became an apostle in his own right. We have modern apostles, prophets, evangelists, pastors, and teachers to help us grow in the likeness of Christ and in the unity of the body of Christ.[180] So we really have no excuse for not walking with God as faithfully as Noah did.

"Let's look at a few more Scriptures about walking with God and then I think we'll be done. Read Psalm 89:15."

"Blessed are the people who know the joyful sound! They walk, O Lord, in the light of Your countenance."[181]

"Walking in the 'light of [God's] countenance' means that His face is turned toward us. That is a picture of intimacy and favor. Now, Amos 3:3."

"Can two walk together, unless they are agreed?"[182]

"Walking with God means being in agreement with God: agreement that His will is best, His ways are best, His counsel is best, and His government is best. It means being convinced that everything that God does is true and right and just. Being in agreement with God means learning not to question God. No one in the Bible who questioned God ever fulfilled their full and ultimate destiny. Agreeing with God means being like Mary, who said, 'Behold the maidservant of the Lord! Let it be to me according to your word,'[183] and not like Zacharias, who was mute for nine months because he would not believe the word from the Lord that he and his wife Elizabeth would have a son, John the Baptist.[184] Now read Micah 4:5."

"For all people walk each in the name of his god, but we will walk in the name of the Lord our God forever and ever."[185]

"Walking with God means walking in His name; in other words, living to honor Him just as obedient children seek to bring honor to their parents and to their family name. We are part of the family of God, and we should live and conduct ourselves accordingly. Read Malachi 2:6."

"The law of truth was in his mouth, and injustice was not found on his lips. He walked with Me in peace and equity, and turned many away from iniquity."[186]

"This verse describes the nature and character of one who walks with God: truthful, just, peaceful, equitable, and committed to bringing others to God.

"Let's turn now to a few promises the Bible gives to those who walk with God. Read Revelation 3:4."

"You have a few names even in Sardis who have not defiled their garments; and they shall walk with Me in white, for they are worthy."[187]

"Throughout the Bible, the color white is used as a symbol of purity. Walking with God means living a lifestyle of purity and holiness. Revelation 21:3."

"And I heard a loud voice from heaven saying, 'Behold, the tabernacle of God is with men, and He will dwell with them, and they shall be His people. God Himself will be with them and be their God.'"[188]

"Do you see how close and intimate God wants to be with us? He has planned all of creation, and especially the creation of the human race, just so He can have us close to Him! Read Isaiah 49:15-16."

"Can a woman forget her nursing child, and not have compassion on the son of her womb? Surely they may forget, yet I will not forget you. See, I have inscribed you on the palms of My hands; your walls are continually before Me."[189]

"God says that He will not forget us and that He has carved us onto the palms of His hands. How much closer can you get? Finally, let's look at John 15:13-15."

"Greater love has no one than this, than to lay down one's life for his friends. You are My friends if you do whatever I command you. No longer do I call you servants, for a servant does not know what his master is doing; but I have called you friends, for all things that I heard from My Father I have made known to you."[190]

"Jesus said that there is no greater love than to lay down one's life for his friends. He proved it when He laid down His life for us on the cross. When we lay down our lives for Him in obedience, we prove our love for Him. Walking with God means being His *friend*. Not everyone who is born again is automatically God's friend in this sense. Our friendship with God is determined by our obedience. If we say we are His friend, we will obey His commands. At the same time, being a friend of God means being a member of His family—His son or daughter by faith.

"Walking with God is not based on feelings. Sometimes we will feel like it and sometimes we won't. That's just the way life is. We do not know that God is real because of our emotions or our physical sensations; we know He is real because we believe. Sometimes the biggest hindrances to our faith are our emotions and our five senses. We walk by faith, not by sight, and in that faith we know that God is real, that He wants us to walk in fellowship with Him, and that He has invited us to be His friend."

"Invited to be God's friend!" Randy repeated in a tone of wonder. "How could there be any greater destiny, any higher purpose for us than that?"

"There isn't," Eli replied. "That's what we were created for; what God intended from the very beginning."

———————

Randy and Eli fell silent and listened to the stream flowing by behind them. After a few moments Eli said, "Well, Randy, that just about wraps it up. Do you have any final questions?"

Randy thought for a few seconds, then shook his head. "No, I'm fine on everything. You've been a fine teacher and I have learned so much these past few days. Thank you."

Eli smiled. "It's good students that make good teachers, and you are one of the best I've had."

Randy returned the smile. "So what's next?" he asked.

They stood up and began walking back toward the cottage.

"It's time for us to return home."

"There's something about this place that makes me want to stay."

"I know; I feel it too, every time I come here. But this place is not intended to be a permanent residence. Think of it like a retreat where you go for a season of refreshing and to recharge your spiritual batteries, so to speak. Randy, you have been afforded a rare and wonderful privilege. I hope you will carry its memories and its lessons with you forever."

"I certainly will. These last four days have helped me see my life and my purpose in a whole new light."

By now Eli and Randy had reached the front door of the cottage, which, as it had done on Randy's arrival, opened by itself.

Stepping over the threshold, Randy asked, "How do I get back?"

"Just go back the way you came."

They stood silently for a few seconds longer, and then embraced. "Thanks, Eli," Randy said. "Thanks for everything."

"You're welcome, Randy. May the Lord bless you and keep you all the days of your life. Goodbye."

"Goodbye."

Randy turned and took several steps down the walk and then stopped. He turned to say a final word but the door had already closed.

10

"ALL THESE THINGS SHALL COME TO PASS..."

Randy made his way quickly down the path from the cottage and in a matter of minutes came to the fork in the road. Bearing left he retraced his steps of four days before. Even before he rounded the bend of the hill he could see in the distance the massive hedge through which he had walked when he left Heaven and entered this realm.

As before, the sky above was bright blue and cloudless. Again he heard birds twittering in the trees. Somewhere nearby but out of sight the waters of a stream gurgled by. Randy wondered if it was the same stream that passed behind the orchard at the back of Eli's cottage.

Making rapid progress as before, Randy soon came around the curve in the path and saw ahead of him the copse of trees that formed the leafy canopy under which he had walked after stepping through the heavy wooden door from the balcony of Heaven. Remembering that the door had no latch or handle on the inside, Randy thought, "How am I going to get it open?" It was more a question of curiosity than concern, because he had learned enough about this unusual world to know that things operated differently here than in his world.

As soon as Randy passed under the tree canopy he was reassured to see in the dim light ahead of him the outline of the wooden door. Approaching it, he noted with only mild surprise that an iron latch and handle had appeared where none had been before. Grasping the handle firmly, Randy lifted the latch and pulled the heavy door open.

Raphael was standing just where Randy had left him, with the balcony of Heaven and the bright shimmering earth in the background. It looked as though nothing had changed. Everything was just as Randy remembered it.

"I guess I shouldn't be surprised that you're here or that you knew I was coming," Randy said to the tall archangel.

"Where else would I be, Randy?" Raphael responded. "You only left a moment ago."

Randy started in surprise. "A moment ago! What do you mean? I was gone for *four days!*" Then he remembered. "Oh, right. Time has no meaning here."

Raphael nodded. "Your four days with Eli were but an instant here."

"The absence of normal time relationships here is still hard for me to get used to," Randy said. "Having spent all my life in a finite space-time system, I can't quite comprehend infinity."

"Don't worry, Randy. Someday when you are here to stay, you will have all the time you need."

Randy thought he caught the slightest trace of a smile on Raphael's otherwise completely impassive face. *Was Raphael making a joke?* Randy shook his head at the foolishness of the thought. *No; it couldn't be! Then again…*

"Come with me, Randy," Raphael said as he turned away from the door.

"Where are we going? Are you taking me home?"

"No. There is one more stop you must make, and then you will go home."

Raphael led Randy to another wooden door in the side of the King's palace. "Go inside and wait there, Randy," he said, pointing to the door.

"I suppose you will be waiting for me again?"

Raphael shook his head. "Not this time. You won't need me anymore. When you are through in there, you will be taken home. Goodbye, Randy."

Randy felt a twinge of disappointment that he would not see the big archangel again. "Goodbye, Raphael. Thanks for everything." Raphael nodded slightly, then turned and walked away.

Randy opened the door and walked through. In the few seconds before the door shut behind him, Randy saw that he was in a tiny room that was completely bare: no furnishings of any kind. With the click of the door latch, Randy was plunged into total darkness. He stood silently in the pitch-black room, listening closely and wondering what would happen next. It began very softly and subtly. Just as a subliminal sound gradually rises in intensity until it passes into conscious hearing, Randy became gently aware of a Presence in the room, a Person totally Other from him, yet of a kindred spirit. He began to feel warm and at the same time the room began to glow with a truly unearthly light that grew quickly into the brightest and most brilliant illumination that he had ever seen, yet it did not hurt his eyes.

Randy recognized the warmth now. It was the same warm benevolence that had so thoroughly permeated his being when He had seen the King in the throne room. Once again Randy's spirit leapt inside as a tidal wave of absolute purest love swept over him. In awe and reverence he fell to his knees on the stone floor, and then to his face, prostrate before his King.

When the Voice spoke, it seemed to surround and envelop Randy and yet bubbled up from inside him at the same time. It was everywhere and he felt and heard it with every fiber of his being.

"Randy."

"Yes, Lord?" Randy's voice was barely a whisper.

"I have loved you with an everlasting love and I have chosen you for My purpose."

"Who am I, Lord, that you would choose me?"

"You have a humble heart and a teachable spirit."

"What would you have me do, Lord?"

"Behold your destiny!"

Suddenly, images grew in Randy's mind. Laid out before him as in an open vision, he saw his philosophy class and himself standing before them. Although there was no sound and the vision played before him like a silent movie, Randy knew in his spirit that he was addressing his class on the theme of the purpose of man. His classmates and his philosophy professor were seated before him, rapt in his words and totally awestruck. Backed by the authority of God's Word, the logic of his arguments tore down every barrier and answered every objection.

The scene changed. Randy was seated at a table stacked high with books. On the cover he could read the title: *Who Am I and Why Am I Here?* He was signing book after book as the line of patrons stretched through the door of the bookstore and out of sight.

Again the scene changed. Randy stood behind a lectern in a stadium filled to capacity with tens of thousands of people hanging on his every word. Above him hung a banner with the words: "God created you for a purpose!"

Each successive image, more compelling than the last, sent shudders of awe and holy fear through Randy's body. Then he heard the Voice speak once again.

"All these things shall come to pass if you will only follow Me."

Silence. Overwhelmed by the power of the vision, Randy could not speak.

Again the Voice echoed in every cell of his body. "Whom shall I send, and who will go for Us?"

Randy's body trembled with excitement as he recognized the words from Isaiah 6:8 and he finally managed to whisper the response: "Here am I! Send me."

"Go and tell My people of My love. Tell them of the great and glorious purposes that I have for them. Drive away the doubts and confusion and hopelessness of lives without meaning. Tell them of the plans I have for them since before the foundation of the world. Go, and I will be with you."

The Voice fell silent, but its final words, "Go, and I will be with you," reverberated in Randy's brain as the light intensified even more and he moved upward and outward into unconsciousness.

Randy slowly lifted his head. He was seated at his desk in his dorm room, his notebook open in front of him. Except for his desk lamp, the room was dark and it was dark outside. Images and thoughts and memories swirled in his head: Raphael, the earth spinning backward, dinosaurs, lucifer being flung from Heaven, the great palace of the King, a strange country where it never rained, Eli, a voice that said, "All these things shall come to pass..."

Randy looked around. Rain still pelted the windows, although lighter than before. He rubbed his eyes. "Wow! What an amazing, incredible dream!" he said aloud. "How long have I been asleep?" He glanced at the clock: 2:30. An uneasy feeling gripped the pit of his stomach. Surely he hadn't slept for 24 hours! He checked the date and time on his computer and couldn't believe his eyes. It was the same night! No time had passed.

How is that possible? It all seemed so real! How could I have such a vivid and detailed dream in only an instant of time? Suddenly, Raphael's words came to mind: "Your four days with Eli were but an instant here." Randy shook his head. *No, it can't be! It was only a dream.*

Randy started to stand up when his eyes fell on his open notebook. He saw the last notes he had taken before falling asleep. His pulse quickened and his body tingled all over as he saw also the notes that followed: pages and pages of notes about eight reasons why God created man—everything he had learned from Raphael and Eli—notes written apparently in his own hand, yet he had no recollection of writing any of it!

He turned over the last page of notes. With a shock that literally took his breath away, his eyes fell on the final entry, written in a hand that was distinctly *not* his own:

"All these things shall come to pass if you will only follow Me."

Many seconds passed as Randy, utterly dumbfounded, stared at the words. Finally, he found his voice. "Then it really *is* true! It really *did* happen! All of it: Raphael, the time travel, Heaven, the King's palace, the Eden-like world, Eli." Images of his vision returned to his mind, and his sense of the Presence overwhelmed him once more. Bowing his head, Randy said, "Here am I! Send me. Yes, Lord! *Send me!*"

The lateness of the hour forgotten, Randy grabbed his notes, turned to his computer and, under the fire of inspiration and the power of his call, began to write in detail about the eight divine purposes of man on the earth.

Several hours later, Randy sat back and stretched. A warm glow of satisfaction filled his spirit. "For the first time in my life," he spoke aloud, "I know who I really am and why I am here. I have a sense of direction and purpose as never before!" He laughed with joy. "It's a great feeling!"

Raising his arms toward Heaven, Randy prayed, "Thank You, Father, for giving me this insight into *Your purpose for creating me*. I now understand and appreciate that it was Your core nature of love that prompted You to create mankind. Here and now, I offer You my life; fulfill Your purpose in me! Grant me the ability to communicate to others the enlightenment You have given me. My life is Yours; do with me as You will."

Randy sensed a voice in his spirit. "Your prayer has been answered. All these things shall come to pass if you will only follow Me. There is much more for you still to learn. You must learn what the Scripture means that says:

'For the earnest expectation of the creation eagerly waits for the revealing of the sons of God. For the creation was subjected to futility, not willingly, but because of Him who subjected it in hope; because the creation itself also will be delivered from the bondage of corruption into the glorious liberty of the children of God. For we know that the whole creation groans and labors with birth pangs together until now.'[191]

"You must also learn the meaning of Paul's words:

'Now to Him who is able to do exceedingly abundantly above all that we ask or think, according to the power that works in us, to Him be glory in the church by Christ Jesus throughout all ages, world without end. Amen.'"[192]

Wow! *Randy thought.* I guess there is a lot more I need to learn about the deeper mysteries of God and His eternal purpose. I wonder if He might someday grant me another visit with Eli in that wonderful place where we first met! *Randy's heart beat faster at the very thought of it.* Why not? If the infinite God could reveal this much about His purpose that I did not know, just think how much more He still has to reveal!

Fired with fresh energy in anticipation of what lay ahead, Randy returned to his notes and continued writing.

ENDNOTES

1. Although the Bible does not mention an archangel named Raphael, an archangel by that name does appear in some of the Jewish apocalyptic literature of the postexilic period. Rather than use the well known archangels mentioned in the Bible, Michael and Gabriel, we chose an unknown name which may not be or maybe the name of one of God's many archangels. The name is used here simply for narrative purposes.

2. Genesis 1:1.

3. Genesis 1:2.

4. Genesis 1:3.

5. Genesis 1:4a.

6. Genesis 1:4b-5.

7. Genesis 1:6.

8. Genesis 1:8a.

9. Genesis 1:9.

10. Genesis 1:10.

11. Genesis 1:11.

12. Genesis 1:12b.

13. Genesis 1:14-15.

14. Genesis 1:16.

15. Genesis 1:18-19.

16. Genesis 1:20.

17. Genesis 1:21.

18. Genesis 1:24.

19. Genesis 1:26.

20. Genesis 2:7a.

21. Genesis 2:7b.

22. Genesis 1:28-29.

23. Genesis 2:15-17.

24. Genesis 2:18.

25. Genesis 2:21-23.

26. Genesis 3:1-6.

27. Genesis 3:7-8.

28. Genesis 1:26-28.

29. John 4:24.

30. John 1:1-3.

31. Genesis 3:22-24.

32. Genesis 2:7-9.

33. Genesis 2:16-17.

34. Genesis 3:17b-19.

35. Philippians 3:20b-21a.

36. Acts 24:15.

37. Daniel 12:2.

38. Romans 5:12, 18.

39. 1 Corinthians 15:21-22.

40. Revelation 20:4-6.

41. Revelation 20:11-15.

42. Genesis 5:24.

43. Hebrews 11:5 NKJV.

44. Genesis 6:5-7, 11-12.

45. Genesis 6:8-9, 13-14, 17-18.

46. Genesis 9:1.

47. Judges 21:25b.

48. Ezekiel 22:30.

49. Isaiah 59:16.

50. 1 Corinthians 15:20.

51. Ephesians 2:11-18.

52. John 3:3;5-6.

53. 2 Corinthians 5:17.

54. 1 Peter 1:18-19.

55. 1 John 1:7b.

56. Colossians 1:21-22.

57. Romans 8:28-29.

58. Ephesians 4:11-13, 15-16.

59. Genesis 4:2b-7.

60. Hebrews 10:8-14.

61. Romans 3:24-25a.

62. 1 John 4:10.

63. Acts 4:12.

64. Phillis Engelbert and Diane L. Dupuis, *The Handy Space Answer Book* (Detroit, MI: Visible Ink Press, a division of Gale Research, 1998), 59.

65. Engelbert and Dupuis, *The Handy Space Answer Book*, 128.

66. Engelbert and Dupuis, *The Handy Space Answer Book*, 137.

67. Engelbert and Dupuis, *The Handy Space Answer Book*, 106.

68. Hugh Ross, *The Fingerprint of God* (New Kensington, PA: Whitaker House, 1989), 130.

69. Hugh Ross, *The Fingerprint of God*, 121-22.

70. Psalm 139:7-10.

71. John 15:13.

72. Hebrews 2:5-10.

73. Genesis 3:6.

74. Genesis 2:17b.

75. Emery H. Bancroft, *Christian Theology* (Grand Rapids, MI: Zondervan Publishing House, 1977), 185.

76. James 1:2-5.

77. James 1:2-5 (Phillips).

78. Romans 8:28-29a.

79. 2 Corinthians 4:15-17.

80. Job 1:8.

81. Genesis 22:12, emphasis added.

82. Hebrews 12:5-11.

83. 1 Corinthians 3:11-15.

84. John 5:17, 19.

85. Philippians 3:10-11.

86. Philippians 3:13b-14.

87. Genesis 2:5b-6.

88. Psalm 2:7.

89. Isaiah 9:6-7.

90. 1 Kings 9:5.

91. John 14:9.

92. Luke 1:31, 35.

93. John 1:1-5.

94. John 1:12-14.

95. John 3:3, 5-7.

96. John 1:18.

97. Galatians 6:15.

98. Romans 8:28-30.

99. Galatians 3:26-29.

100. Romans 8:15-17.

101. 2 Timothy 3:12.

102. Hebrews 2:10.

103. Isaiah 56:5.

104. Acts 11:26.

105. Psalm 45:9.

106. Song of Songs 4:8-12; 5:1.

107. Isaiah 49:16.

108. Isaiah 61:10.

109. Isaiah 62:5.

110. John 3:28-30.

111. Romans 7:4.

112. 2 Corinthians 11:2.

113. Revelation 19:7.

114. Revelation 21:1-2.

115. Revelation 21:9-11a.

116. Genesis 2:23-24.

117. Ephesians 1:3-4.

118. Titus 1:2.

119. Paul E. Billheimer, *Destined for the Throne* (Fort Washington, PA: Christian Literature Crusade, 1975), 22.

120. Ephesians 5:22-32.

121. 1 Corinthians 6:17.

122. 1 Corinthians 12:13a.

123. Matthew 7:13-14.

124. Dr. Bill Hamon, *The Eternal Church* (Shippensburg, PA: Destiny Image Publishers, Inc., 1981, rev. ed. 2003), 332-3.

125. Hebrews 12:2.

126. Dr. Bill Hamon, *The Eternal Church*, 18-19.

127. 1 Corinthians 2:9.

128. Dr. Bill Hamon, *Prophets and the Prophetic Movement* (Shippensburg, PA: Destiny Image Publishers, Inc., 1990), 95.

129. 1 Corinthians 15:26.

130. 1 Thessalonians 4:16-17.

131. Revelation 21:7.

132. Matthew 25:34.

133. John 15:13.

134. Acts 20:28.

135. Ephesians 5:25-27.

136. 1 John 2:22.

137. 1 John 4:3.

138. 2 Timothy 3:5.

139. Hebrews 9:22.

140. Ephesians 2:19-21.

141. 1 Corinthians 3:11.

142. Matthew 16:13-18.

143. Dr. Bill Hamon, *The Eternal Church*, 29.

144. Revelation 12:7-9.

145. Exodus 8:32.

146. Exodus 9:12.

147. Exodus 10:1-2.

148. Exodus 14:1-4.

149. Exodus 14:13-14.

150. 1 Corinthians 12:4-14.

151. Ephesians 4:11-16.

152. 2 Corinthians 5:19.

153. Matthew 25:14-30.

154. Matthew 28:19-20.

155. 1 Peter 1:12.

156. Revelation 4:1-11.

157. Ephesians 1:12.

158. Hebrews 13:15-16.

159. John 4:20-24.

160. John 14:6.

161. Romans 12:1.

162. Romans 12:1b NAS.

163. Acts 2:42.

164. 1 Corinthians 1:9.

165. Galatians 2:9.

166. Philippians 2:1-2.

167. Philippians 3:10.

168. Luke 9:23.

169. 1 John 1:3-7.

170. Matthew 18:20.

171. Genesis 3:8.

172. Genesis 5:24.

173. Hebrews 11:6.

174. 2 Corinthians 5:7.

175. 2 John 1:4.

176. Ephesians 5:2.

177. Galatians 5:16.

178. Genesis 6:5-9.

179. Romans 8:34.

180. Ephesians 4:11-13.

181. Psalm 89:15.

182. Amos 3:3.

183. Luke 1:38.

184. Luke 1:20.

185. Micah 4:5.

186. Malachi 2:6.

187. Revelation 3:4.

188. Revelation 21:3.

189. Isaiah 49:15-16.

190. John 15:13-15.

191. Romans 8:19-22.

192. Ephesians 3:20-21.

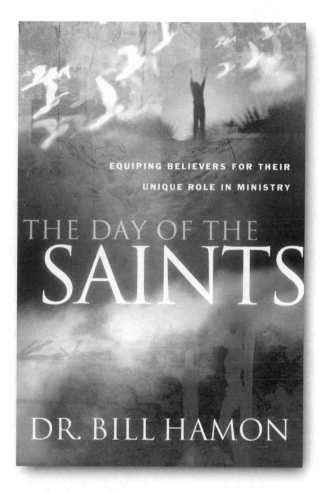

THE DAY OF THE SAINTS

Many Christians are looking for 'the Day of the Lord' but before that day comes the Lord is preparing His Bride for His Divine purposes in the earth. All creation longs for that day—*The Day of the Saints*. It is on God's prophetic timetable and is the day when the Saints will fulfill all the Scriptures regarding Christ's glorious Church.

0-7684-2166-7

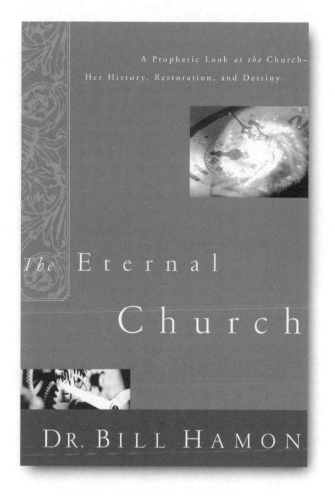

THE ETERNAL CHURCH

This unique perspective shows graphically the whys as well as the whats of church history. Bill Hamon is a valid modern prophet who writes the story of the Church of Jesus Christ from the perspective of one who sees not only the past, but has glimpses into the future.

0-7684-2176-4

Available at your local Christian bookstore.

For more information and sample chapters, visit www.destinyimage.com

Additional copies of this book and other
book titles from DESTINY IMAGE are
available at your local bookstore.

For a bookstore near you, call 1-800-722-6774

Send a request for a catalog to:

Destiny Image® Publishers, Inc.

P.O. Box 310
Shippensburg, PA 17257-0310

*"Speaking to the Purposes of God for This
Generation and for the Generations to Come"*

For a complete list of our titles,
visit us at www.destinyimage.com

914
3782